The Freshwater Angler™

ULTRALIGHT FISHING

Tim Lilley

CREATIVE
PUBLISHING
international

CHANHASSEN, MINNESOTA

www.creativepub.com

TIM LILLEY'S articles and photographs have been published in magazines such as *Fins & Feathers, Fur-Fish-Game, In-Fisherman, Game & Fish*. Tim has been fishing the ultralight way since grade school when he received an ultralight rig for his birthday. The next smallmouth he caught made him a believer and he's never gone back to his old ways. He lives in Athens, Georgia.

ACKNOWLEDGMENTS

I started to call this book a labor of love, but it wasn't labor at all. Just like its topic, is was pure fun. My editor at CPI, Barbara Harold, is a major reason for that. Thank you, Barbara!

Another editor I've worked with for many years was the catalyst for this book. Thank you Nick Gilmore, for your friendship and your confidence in my work over the years.

The following people have been major influences on my life. I thank them all and dedicate this book to them in gratitude:

My parents; my daughter Jennifer; Jim Galusky and his sons Steve, Ernie and Jamie; Jim Givens; Ralph Schlagel; James "Lash" Nesser; Leslie Lovett; Richard Brady; Charlie and Carolyn Heartwell; Jack Bell; Rev. Dr. Stacy Groscup; Mike Walker; Ham Hamberger; Ted C. Tow; Bill Seymour; Randy Worsham; Dan and Stacey Delcour; Ken Chaumont; Larry Colombo; John L. Morris; Steve Holland; Carol Robinson; Kevin VanDam; Rick Clunn; Woo Daves; Gene Hacker; Mark Firestone; Gary Giudice; Lisa McDowell-Snuggs.

Copyright © 2005 by Creative Publishing international, Inc.
18705 Lake Drive East
Chanhassen, MN 55317
1-800-328-3895
www.creativepub.com

President/CEO: Ken Fund
Vice President/Publisher: Linda Ball
Vice President/Retail Sales & Marketing: Kevin Haas
Executive Editor, Outdoor Group: Barbara Harold
Creative Director: Brad Springer
Project Manager: Tracy Stanley
Photo Editor: Angela Hartwell
Production Manager: Laura Hokkanen

Printed in China
10 9 8 7 6 5 4 3 2 1

ULTRALIGHT FISHING
by Tim Lilley

Cover Photo: Bill Lindner Photography/blpstudio.com
Photo on page 116: West Virginia Division of Tourism; Steve Shaluta/WV Tourism.
Contributing Photographers: Bill Buckley, Mark Emery, Tim Lilley, Bill Lindner, David J. Sams, Dusan Smetana, Dale Spartas, Doug Stamm.

Contributing Manufacturers: Arbogast Lures, Bass Pro Shops, Berkley, Bill Lewis Lures, Blakemore Lure Company, Blue Fox, Bomber, Booyah Bait Company, Cotton Cordell, Daiwa Corporation, Dardevle, Eagle Claw, Heddon Lures, Johnson, Kalin Company, Lazy Ike Lures, Lindy, Luhr-Jensen & Sons, Mann's Bait Company, Mepps, The Orvis Company, P-Line, Panther Martin, Quantum, Rapala, Rebel, St. Croix, Sage Manufacturing, Shakespeare Fishing Tackle, Shimano American Corporation, Slug-Go, Smithwick, Storm Lures, Stren, Terminator, Worden's Lures, Gary Yamamoto Custom Baits, Yo-Zuri America Inc., Yum, Zebco.

Library of Congress Cataloging-in-Publication Data

Lilley, Tim
  Ultralight fishing / Tim Lilley.
      p. cm.
  Includes index.
  ISBN 1-58923-199-6 (hardcover)
  1. Fishing tackle. I. Title.
  SH447.L55 2005
  688.7'91--dc22

                                    2004021161

TABLE OF CONTENTS

Introduction 4

Equipment Options

Chapter 1 Tackle—What You Need to Succeed 6

Chapter 2 Lures—There Are More Than You Think! 22

Chapter 3 Water—Read It and See Fish 34

UL Works on All Fish

Chapter 4 Bass 44

Chapter 5 Crappies and Other Panfish 58

Chapter 6 Pike and Muskies .70

Chapter 7 Catfish 82

Chapter 8 Trout 90

Ride or Walk?

Chapter 9 Trolling 104

Chapter 10 Fly Fishing 112

Afterword 122
Manufacturer Sources 123
Index 126

You don't need heavy tackle to catch heavy fish.

Introduction

I hope to show anglers everywhere how true that statement is.

Along the way, you're going to read some things that will challenge your thinking about what ultralight fishing really is all about. It's not always about the shortest, lightest and tiniest rods, reels and baits you can get your hands on. This type of fishing challenges you to do everything right on every cast. It forces you to become the best angler you can be.

Throughout this book, you're going to read about tackle, baits and techniques that, by their very nature, will increase your odds of hooking fish. They also could decrease your chances of landing those fish because they may

be lighter than optimum for actually getting fish into your net or boat.

Also, match your equipment to the fish for another very important reason: You don't want to go so light that the fight to land it jeopardizes the future health of any fish you release.

Before reading on, take a minute to answer the following three questions:

1. Which species do you think of when you hear the term ultralight?
2. How long is the rod you'd expect to use?
3. How heavy are the line and lure you'd expect to use?

Your answers probably are similar to these:

If you live in a coldwater climate, the species that come to mind are probably going to be trout, yellow perch or bluegills. In warmwater regions, they'll be crappies or other sunfish.

In either case, the rod you envision probably isn't longer than 5 feet (1.5 m), and it's a spinning rod. You see it casting line no heavier than 4-pound-test (1.8-kg), with lures weighing no more than 1/8 ounce (3.5 g); probably less.

Unfortunately, all of those presumptions suggest you can only go ultralight in certain situations, and only for certain fish. Nothing could be further from the truth!

In this book, ultralight defines a state of mind more than specific tackle or lures. Sure, there have to be some boundaries, but they don't have to be quite so restrictive. In most of the chapters that follow, the line-weight limit will be 6-pound-test (2.7-kg), and lures will weigh no more than 1/4 ounce (7 g). There won't be any length limit on rods, even for fly fishing.

Among the elements you may find most surprising are my suggestions of longer rods for spinning and shorter rods for fishing dry flies. In these and many other areas, the information in this book is intended to open your eyes to a world of ultralight fishing that is much broader, much more diverse, than you may think.

Although you'll read about them, this book isn't just about catching native brook trout from tiny mountain streams or scrappy sunfish from farm ponds. More than anything, it's about how you can change your approach to fishing. You can become more versatile, more successful and more excited about every fishing trip—with less tackle, less weight and less failure.

Throughout this book, you'll read accounts of my encounters with fish and the ultralight lessons they taught me. They occurred on streams and lakes of various size in Arkansas, Kansas, Missouri, Pennsylvania and West Virginia. But don't make the mistake of thinking that the tackles, lures and tactics described here will only work in those places.

From the farthest reaches and most remote of Canadian waters to the trout streams of "Big Sky Country" in the American West, from weed-choked southern bass ponds to the deep and gin-clear reservoirs of Arizona and California, fish are fish. They all need the same things: primarily, cover and food. What you read about those two elements in this book will apply no matter where you fish.

Are you going to Canada after smallmouth this season? Or will you have a chance to visit some other great fishery while traveling on business or during a family vacation? If so, you can experience some great ultralight fishing. You'll just have to do a little homework.

Before leaving home, get as much information as you can on the lake or stream you'll visit. Know what species are available, and think about the time of year and what the fish are doing. Then, select your tackle and lures. That's the magic of ultralight fishing; it works anywhere, just about any time.

When it comes to fishing with ultralight gear, these are the good old days. Thanks to wise management and the success of catch-and-release, you have more and bigger fish in more places than at any other time in modern history. Manufacturers have responded by bringing to market the best and most diverse selection of tackle and baits ever.

No matter which species of fish you enjoy most, you can find the right ultralight combination to catch it. And no matter which style of fishing you prefer, there is ultralight gear out there you can easily adapt to that style.

You won't have to learn anything new. Instead, you'll take a new, fresh look at everything you already do on the water. Some of the ideas here will strike you as unorthodox—like using a 7-foot (2.1-m) spinning rod on a little trout stream or a closed-face spincasting reel on your favorite bass rod. But they work for me, and they'll work for you.

Without question, the mental aspect of ultralight fishing is one of its most important elements. This book will show you how to use many of the techniques you already use in many of the places you already cast to take heavy fish on tackle that's lighter—maybe much lighter—than what you're used to using.

In the process, you'll begin focusing on the details that will improve your catch ratio. You'll pay more attention to knots, to your reel's drag setting, to the kinds of casts you make and how even a subtle change in presentation can make a big difference in fooling more fish more often. You'll have as many choices in baits and tackle as you're used to. But all of them will be lighter, and that will provide you with a bigger, more rewarding challenge every time you hit the water.

That's exactly what makes ultralight fishing so much fun!

Chapter 1

Tackle: What You Need to Succeed

When it comes to rods, reels, lines and lures, ultralight fishing is relative. For every species covered in this book except for the largest pike, muskies and catfish, the examples will be consistent and fairly simple.

Throughout this book, the term ultralight (UL) will apply to lures that weigh 1/4 ounce (7 g) or less. The only exceptions you'll find to that weight limit will be in the chapter on lightening up for pike and muskies. But even there, you'll see it's possible to fool some of the largest, most aggressive freshwater gamefish species available on lures as light as 1/4 ounce (7 g).

Regardless of the relative weight of the gear you're using, there are a couple of general principles that always apply:

• Longer rods help you make longer casts.

• Heavier line helps slow down the rate of a bait's fall; lighter line speeds it up.

So even though you're shedding weight in your rod rack and tackle box, you'll still have to plan your approach to yield the most success.

Rods

Maybe the most important thing to understand is that you don't have to use the smallest, shortest rods you can find to be practicing ultralight fishing. Sometimes those rods marketed as UL might just put you at a disadvantage when it comes to catching fish all the time with UL gear.

Disadvantage? Absolutely.

Many times, the smallest rods you can buy will complicate casting. For example, you might not be able to make the presentation you need to get to the fish you're after because your rod's not long enough.

Recent fishing seasons have seen me spending quite a bit of time chasing trout on the very

upper reaches of the Youghiogheny River, in Garrett County, Maryland. The Yough (pronounced *Yawk*) flows north through Garrett County and into Pennsylvania, where it offers rafters and kayakers some of the finest whitewater opportunities in the East.

Where I fish it, however, the Yough more closely resembles some of the lazy, meandering smallmouth streams I fished for a decade or so while living

The Upper Youghiogheny River in Maryland may require using rods in the 6-foot range rather than the smaller UL rods to get around vegetation and over high banks.

in Missouri. Its bottom is more soft silt than rock along the sections I fish, but still cool enough to support the rainbow and brown trout stocked throughout the year by the Maryland Department of Natural Resources.

A couple of hours south, in West Virginia's Monongahela National Forest, you find streams about the same size that are the stereotypical eastern freestone trout flows. Their courses take them through and down the mountains, with significant altitude changes and lots of pools and deep runs. But here, along the Yough, some of the best trout-holding spots are areas where the river flows along the edges of pasturelands, with steep, soft banks that are lined with lush, healthy vegetation.

Unlike those West Virginia trout streams I often visit, this section of the Yough challenges anglers to reach the best fish-holding locations by making casts over and around that vegetation. And when fish are hooked, landing them can mean bringing them up several feet of bank while keeping them out of the weeds and brush.

And you know what? A 4$\frac{1}{2}$-foot (1.4-m) ultralight rod is impossible to use in a situation like that. It just won't work. You need a rod at least a foot (30 cm) longer—a tool that will let you retrieve your lures and land hooked fish by lifting them from the water on the outside of the vegetation and getting them above it.

On those West Virginia streams, however, the shorter rod usually works just fine because you're going to be either wading in the stream, over a hard, rocky bottom; or you'll be along the edges, which are not as consistently steep and brush-strewn.

Let's switch our thinking to still water. From the shores of most ponds or lakes, or from a boat, you again won't have the kind of obstructions that will make the shortest of UL rods nearly impossible to use.

However, you also won't have the ability to make the kind of long casts that longer rods provide. And when it comes to fishing lakes, covering water is a big part of the game. Longer rods are the best way to go for that reason.

St. Croix's line in the Avid Series of spinning rods comes in lengths from 5' to 8' for ultralight to medium-light fishing.

Quantum 6$\frac{1}{2}$', 2-piece spinning rod in the Xtralite series

TACKLE: WHAT YOU NEED TO SUCCEED

Spinning Rods

Make no mistake, you have more choices in spinning rods than in any other category. You can get them as short as 4½ feet (1.4 m) and as long as 7 feet (2.1 m), all capable of handling lures weighing no more than ¼ ounce (7 g).

Virtually every rod maker offers at least one spinning model that truly is UL in nature. They generally are rated to handle lines up to 6-pound-test (2.7-kg), and lures up to either ⅛ or ¼ ounce (3.5 or 7 g). These lightest of rods won't be longer than 5½ feet (1.7 m), and most will be 5 (1.5 m). A few will be shorter; one example is the 4½-foot (1.4-m) Shakespeare Ugly Stik.

I have a few really short rods like that; and over the years, I

have come to use them less and less. Once you've handled a truly balanced UL outfit that features a longer rod, these short ones start feeling as awkward and difficult to cast accurately as anything you'll use.

Think about this: On even the smallest of native brook trout streams, a long spinning or casting rod does not put you at a disadvantage because, unlike fly fishing, you don't have to false-cast. Long rods on narrow streams actually help you make precise presentations.

For instance, during a late-spring visit to another western Maryland trout fishery, the Middle Fork of the Savage River, I encountered the kind of low, clear water you normally expect to find on this medium-size native brookie stream in late

August, not late May. But find it I did; and I was glad to have a 6½-foot (1.98-m) spinning rod with me.

That extra length made it possible for me to actually "dabble" my spinners into a couple of spots—that is, to position myself so that I could get the rod tip right over the spot I wanted to start fishing the lure, then just let it drop softly into the water. In a situation where making a delicate presentation with a short rod would have been tough at best, the long rod saved the day.

As mentioned earlier, the rods you find in the 4½- to 5½-foot (1.4- to 1.7-m) range generally are going to be true ultralight models, designed for use with the lightest of lines and baits. Finding a longer rod that balances

Eagle Claw Featherlight Series of spinning rods comes in lengths from 5' to 7' and 1 or 2 sections

Shakespeare Ugly Stik Lite 4' 6" spinning rod

Rapala Tournament Class Series 6' medium-light spinning rod

properly for this kind of fishing takes a little more research. However, more rod makers are bringing longer, lighter rods to market every season.

Here's my rule of thumb for a long UL spinning rod: I look for rods that are rated to handle line ranges of either 2- to 8-pound-test (0.9- to 3.6-kg), or 4- to 10-pound-test (1.8- to 4.5-kg). These often are sold as "light-action" rods instead of UL; however, once you've assembled a properly balanced outfit, I believe you'll achieve a feel almost identical to a short UL rig, but with the advantages that the longer rod offers.

I prefer two-piece rods because they are easily stowed behind the seat of my pickup. That way, I can keep a UL rig and some baits handy, and take advantage of fishing opportunities that might present themselves unexpectedly. One-piece rods are usually at least a little bit more sensitive, but I trade that for the convenience of multi-piece rods in longer lengths.

Rod Action

Generally a concept reserved for flyrods, rod action can come into play when we start talking about expanding rod selection beyond the shortest and lightest of UL rods.

Where you find it listed, rod action usually falls into one of four categories—slow, moderate, fast or extremely fast. Each is a measure of how far down from the tip you get significant flex in the rod. The slower the action, the more flex it has. The "wimpiest" feeling rods are those with the slowest actions. That doesn't mean they won't handle the biggest fish you can catch. It just means that they'll feel softer. Heck, thirty years ago, most everything was fiberglass, and all those rods were slow. Action definitely is a relative term.

And this UL fanatic is definitely happy that technology is catching up to the ultralight world because I like fast-action rods. Always have. In my hand, the less flex, the better the rod feels. There are times when, admittedly, this can be a disadvantage.

If you bass fish, especially with crankbaits, you know that fiberglass has made a major comeback over the past decade because those rods' designs are inherently slower than the more modern graphite rods, and that slower action can be an advantage when fishing crankbaits. The slower rods cause anglers to react slightly slower to strikes; and when fishing crankbaits, that actually can be better.

Over the years, however, I have become very fond of the sensitivity and feel provided by fast-action rods, and I prefer them, hands down, regardless of the type of fishing I'm doing. My best advice to you is, before you go shopping for that perfect UL rig or any new rod, take some time to think about the rod(s) you have enjoyed fishing the most over the years. You may discover that, like me, you gravitate toward faster actions. Or, your taste may run toward more moderate or even slower rods.

Rapala 6' medium-light casting rod

Eagle Claw Featherlight 4' 10" casting rod

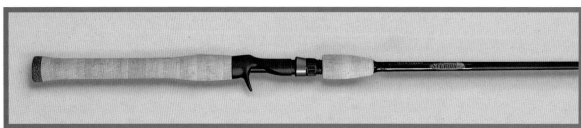

St. Croix casting rod in the Avid Series comes in a 6' 9" length and is for medium-light fishing.

TACKLE: WHAT YOU NEED TO SUCCEED

Remember this: There is no all-encompassing right or wrong answer when it comes to picking your favorite UL rod. It comes down to what feels and works best for you; whatever action it is that gives you the most confidence on the water. That's what you should stick with.

Baitcasting Rods

Up to this point, I've talked only about spinning rods—with good reason. Hardly anybody makes a good UL baitcasting rod—especially a long one! And that's a real shame.

Several years ago, there was a 6-foot (1.8-m), one-piece baitcaster in the Quantum line-up that was rated for 4- to 12-pound (1.8- to 5.4-kg) line, and it was a real beauty for the kind of UL bass fishing this book covers. I had one, and used it more than all my other bass rigs combined—until it broke while I was playing a big bass that hit my UL popper.

Age and use claimed this rod. I had it for a half-dozen seasons, and had made thousands

of casts with it. My only disappointment was that I never found a suitable replacement—until recently. In its Premier line of medium-priced rods, St. Croix offers a two-piece, fast-action casting rod that is rated medium-light. It's built to handle 4- to 10-pound (1.8- to 4.5-kg) line, and is rated for lures from 1/8 to 1/2 ounce (3.5 to 14 g). Again, with all due respect to St. Croix, it'll cast a 1/16-ounce (1.7-g) spinner or a 1/10-ounce (2.8-g) UL crankbait all day on 6-pound (2.7-kg) line. And it has the power to handle very large fish. It's a nice rod for the kinds of UL fishing discussed on these pages, and it's a shame more manufacturers don't offer similar models.

Generally, the only baitcasting rods you find are true UL models like the one in the Eagle Claw Featherlight line mentioned earlier. But it's only 4 feet 10 inches (1.5 m) long.

Memo to rod makers: UL rods shouldn't all be short! Few manufacturers seem to understand this.

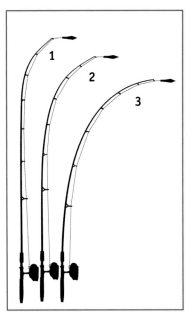

Rod action is shown by pulling equally on different rods of the same power. A fast-action rod (1) bends mainly near the tip; a medium-action (2), over the front half; a slow-action (3), over the entire rod length.

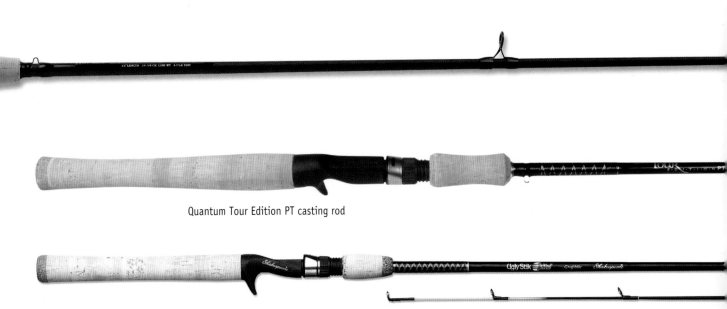

Quantum Tour Edition PT casting rod

Shakespeare Ugly Stik Lite 7', 2-piece ultralight rod

Lots of Brands, Lots of Choices

Bass Pro Shops and Cabela's are two major mail-order retailers of fishing tackle and accessories. Both offer "house brand" rods that fit my UL guidelines. In most cases, these house-brand rods will provide more bang for your buck because they include many of the features found on much higher priced "name brand" rods at a fraction of their retail prices.

Some anglers, however, swear by certain brands, just like some folks have to drive Chevys or Fords or Dodges. Nothing wrong with that. If you have enjoyed good success with certain brands of fishing gear, then by all means, stick with them. Whatever gives you the most confidence is the brand(s) you should stick with.

There are an amazing number of UL rods on the market today, as defined by my guidelines. You will find many more spinning rods to suit the techniques described in this book than you will casting models. But there are more of the latter than you might think. Some of each include:

Spinning Rods

• Eagle Claw makes a Featherlight series of spinning rods from 5 feet (1.5 m) to a whopping 9 feet (2.7 m) long, all rated for line weights from either 2 to 6 pounds (0.9 to 2.7 kg) or 4 to 8 pounds (1.8 to 3.6 kg). And all of them retail for less than $30.00, ranking them among the best buys you'll find.

• G.Loomis has rods up to 7 feet (2.1 m) long in the UL line range. They are much more expensive, but feature a wide range of actions.

• Fenwick's HMG Graphite series includes a number of rods that fit the UL mold, and they carry lifetime limited warranties.

• St. Croix also has several nice UL rods; the model lineup includes multiple price ranges and warranties that vary from two years to lifetime.

• Quantum's Xtralite series of rods is inexpensive and includes some really nice models. I own one of them—the 6 1/2-foot (1.98-m) two-piece model. And with all due respect to the Quantum folks, that rod handles 1/4-ounce (7-g) lures fished on 6-pound (2.7-kg) lines quite well, even though it's rated to only handle lures up to 1/8 ounce (3.5 g).

• Rapala also has gotten into the rod business, and its line of spinning rods includes some nice, medium-priced models that are perfect for the kind of UL bass fishing covered in this book.

Casting Rods

• Cabela's E-Glass line of fiberglass rods includes a 6 1/2-foot (1.98-m) model that's rated to handle lures as light as 1/8 ounce (3.5 g). Its length will help you make longer casts with lighter lures. The forgiving nature of fiberglass also should help you hook more fish when casting crankbaits and spinnerbaits.

• G.Loomis has a 6-foot (1.8-m) IMX Graphite light-action casting rod with a fast action that provides good sensitivity, especially for fishing subsurface baits. Loomis also has a 7-foot (2.1-m) medium-light rod in its crankbait series that provides among the best combinations of casting distance and sensitivity.

• You'll get a lifetime limited warranty with the 6 1/2-foot (1.98-m) Fenwick HMG graphite casting rod that's rated for light action.

• Quantum's Tour Edition PT line includes a 6-foot 4-inch (1.92-m), medium-light casting rod that's rated to handle lures as light as 1/8 ounce (3.5 g). You should be able to use 6-pound (2.7-kg) line on this rod and use lures even lighter.

• Eagle Claw's Featherlight series includes what many anglers would consider a "traditional" UL casting rod; it's only 4 foot 10 inches (1.47 m), and will handle line as light as 2-pound-test (0.9-kg).

• In its Avid line, St. Croix offers a 6-foot 9-inch (2.05-m) casting rod with an extra-fast action rated for medium-light fishing and lines as light as 6 pounds (2.7 kg). This offers another good mix of hook-setting power and sensitivity.

• Shakespeare's popular Ugly Stik line includes a 7-foot (2.1-m) casting rod rated for medium-light fishing. More interesting is the 6-footer (1.8 m) that handles line as light as 6 to 7 pounds (2.7 to 3.2 kg). It's rated at medium-action, which suggests that it might be the perfect choice for bass anglers who like fishing jigs and worms, but who want to lighten up.

This list is not intended to be all-inclusive. But it should give you an idea that, when it comes to high-quality rods that will handle UL fishing as outlined in this book, you don't have to stick with something really short and wimpy-feeling.

Reels

It's easy to argue that reels might just be the most over-looked element of any fishing rig—ultralight, light, heavy, whatever. Many anglers seem to believe that, as long as the reel they have will handle an appropriate length of the weight of line they want to fish, they'll be OK.

They will; but they also could create an outfit that's unbalanced, awkward-feeling and, as a result, more tiring and frustrating to fish than it should be.

Today's reels are stronger and lighter than they've ever been. They have more features and stronger drag systems than ever before. And they're made using materials that include high-tech composite plastics and metals as exotic as titanium.

If you decide to go shopping for a new UL fishing combo, you'll see names as familiar and comfortable as Zebco, Daiwa and Shimano, and as new and unknown (to many anglers) as U.S. Reel and Okuma. Even venerable saltwater names like Penn are getting into the freshwater market, and their offerings include models that fit the UL definitions outlined in this book.

No matter what kind of reel you prefer (spincasting, spinning or baitcasting), you'll be able to find models that will provide you with good quality and plenty of features, at prices that won't break the bank. What follows is a look at each of the major types of UL reels.

Spincasting Reels

Closed-face spincasting reels offer the best options for use on traditional baitcasting rods, and it seems this style of reel is enjoying a resurgence in interest from manufacturers, which is good news for anglers.

It means that you'll find more quality spincasting reels on the market these days. Among the best is one of the oldest models out there—Daiwa's Goldcast series. I've been using the same GC-80, which is the smallest of this line, for more than a decade, and it continues to perform flawlessly. It's built to handle up to 85 yards (77 m) of 8-pound (3.6-kg) line, which makes it perfect for me because I prefer 6-pound (2.7-kg) line. That gets me in the 100-yard (91-m) range when I spool up with the 6.

Johnson, Abu Garcia and Quantum also make high-quality spincasting reels. At one time, Johnson's Citation reels were among the best you could buy of any design, and it's nice to see this design enjoying renewed popularity.

For most of us, a fairly inexpensive Zebco spincasting reel was part of the first fishing outfit we ever owned and used. And just as all UL rods don't have to be short, all spincasting reels don't have to be made cheaply. Many today aren't; and that's more good news.

Daiwa Underspin Gold and Goldcast spincasting reels

Bass Pro Shops Tinylite combo rod and spincast reel sets

Zebco Micro reels

Spinning Reels

Maybe the best news of all, however, when it comes to UL fishing, is the amazingly large number of really high quality open-face spinning reels on the market today that are built to handle 100 yards (91 m) or less of 6-pound (2.7-kg) line. That's the rule of thumb to use when picking a reel to go on your favorite UL rod.

If you decide to buy a good-quality UL rig after reading this book, there's a good chance it's going to be a spinning outfit because that's where you're going to find the most options in rods and reels. I truly wish that wasn't the case, but it is. And all you have to do is look through catalogs to see that there literally are dozens of reels that will fit UL. You'll find them in every price range. And

if you want to assemble an outfit that will last you a lifetime, you can find that kind of quality in one of today's UL spinning rigs.

Reels are smoother than ever, with drag systems that are more efficient than ever. Unless you opt for the absolutely lowest priced reel you can find, you're probably going to get a spare line spool with the reel. I like that. I always carry a spare spool in my pocket when I go stream fishing because you never know what kind of mishap will cause you to lose enough line to make longer casts problematic.

And when compared to baitcasting reels, you're going to get a tremendous bang for your buck with today's spinning reels. For whatever the reason, there are some manufacturers

that seem to believe that if they're going to call it ultra-light, it has to be really small and not as durable as the rest of the products they build and sell. I just still don't get that mindset.

So, I go with slightly larger reels because I want durability. My workhorse UL spinning reel has been a Daiwa SS 700, which is more than ten years old and has never failed to fish when I asked it to. It's not as light or as small as I could go, but it balances well on the longer UL rods I prefer. And it doesn't let me down.

Recently, however, I may have found its replacement: the smallest Quantum Catalyst PTi reel, the No. 10. It's set up for 125 yards (114 m) of 4-pound (1.8-kg) line, which means it'll take all the 6-pound-test (2.7-

Bass Pro Microlite combo rod and spinning reel sets

Daiwa SS Tournament 700

Shimano Symetre 1500FI

kg) I need. It is among the smoothest reels I have ever used, and its magnetic bail system is springless—no bail springs to worry about.

This reel feels perfect on that 6¹/₂-foot (1.98-kg) Xtralite rod mentioned earlier. On a faster-action rod, it'll be part of an amazing UL bass or even pike and muskie rig—although the latter admittedly would be almost featherlight when it comes to those big, toothy critters.

On my shortest of UL spinning rods, I prefer to use triggerspin-style, closed-face reels. I sacrifice some line capacity, but the bails on the really small UL reels seem to be more delicate than I prefer. Johnson, Daiwa and Quantum all make triggerspin reels that fit this kind of outfit just perfectly.

Baitcasting Reels

You'll find very few baitcasting reels that are designed with line capacities that befit UL angling. Based on what's available, you're going to have to opt for baitcasters offering line capacities in the neighborhood of 100 yards (91 m) of 10-pound (4.5-kg) line to get something that will work and, more importantly, balance properly, with a UL baitcasting rod as described here. And there just aren't many of them around.

Among the few that I know of are Shimano's Calcutta TE, which is about the smallest around (models are offered with line capacities of 95 yards/86 m of 8-pound-test/5.4-kg) but also among the most expensive. Daiwa used to make one of

comparable size that was priced lower, but it's been out of their lineup for several years. Most of the currently available baitcasting reels are built with line capacities of more than 100 yards (91 m) of 12-pound-test (5.4-kg).

That tells me that (1) they are going to feel at least a little bulky and awkward on a rod like the St. Croix mentioned earlier, and (2) filling them with lighter line is problematic. You could, if you wanted to, start filling these reels with heavier line; then, once you've got the spool about half full, attach lighter line with a double surgeon's knot or similar knot and finish the process. But to me, that defeats the purpose of UL fishing. It is an option to consider, however.

Quantum Catalyst PTi
spinning reel

Shimano
Calcutta
baitcasting reel

Eagle Claw
Featherlight XG9-10
spinning reel

Daiwa TD SOL
baitcasting reel

Stren monofilament line

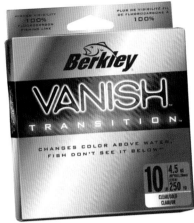

Berkley fluorocarbon line

Yo-Zuri hybrid line

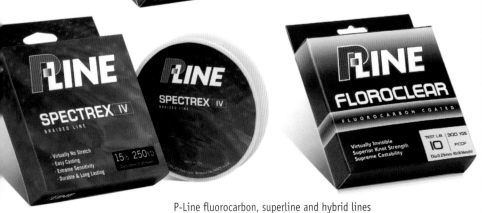

P-Line fluorocarbon, superline and hybrid lines

Line

If there is any one techno-logical development in the fishing industry that I could pinpoint as being most responsible for this book coming to life, it's the improvements in fishing line. Doesn't it seem as if there are as many different kinds of fishing lines these days as there are lures to tie onto them?

When you get right down to it, there are. And they are stronger than ever before. Ultralight fishing isn't nearly as "iffy" a proposition as it was even ten years ago because lighter lines are of higher quality than they've ever been.

Talk about choices. You have monofilaments, fluorocarbons, hybrids that combine monofilament with fluorocarbon, and braided superlines.

Monofilament

This is the most popular line you can find in the lighter weights. Manufacturers continue to improve its tensile strength and abrasion resistance, which are the two most damaging elements when it comes to day-in, day-out fishing. From house brands offered by Bass Pro Shops and Cabela's to the old standbys like Stren and Berkley, you'll find plenty of choices in light monofilament. You'll also find plenty of shades, from clear to photosensitive, which changes shades underwater.

The market also has some other players these days. Brands like P-Line, Maxima, Cajun and Silver Thread are all valid choices for you to look at. I've used practically all of them over the years with fairly good success.

Fluorocarbon

More recently, fluorocarbon line has come along. Its most significant advantage over monofilament is that UV light won't cause it to deteriorate. Other claimed advantages include even higher abrasion resistance than mono, and greater knot strength. It's also said to be virtually invisible underwater, and it doesn't absorb water at all.

Several manufacturers offer fluorocarbon line today, and my hunch is that more will add it to their catalogs as time goes on. Whenever you shop for line, be on the lookout for a fluorocarbon option.

Some of the brands you're likely to find include Berkley, which calls its version Vanish; Seaguar, which makes a product for freshwater anglers it simply designates FW; Silver Thread, which offers a fluorocarbon; and P-Line, whose Soft Fluorocarbon is available as light as 2-pound-test (0.9-kg).

Hybrid

One hybrid line manufactured by Yo-Zuri is a solid line a lot like mono that has a double coating of fluorocarbon. My experience with it suggests that it definitely displays the latter's penchant for greater knot strength. It spools onto reels flawlessly, with virtually no twist or memory. It's easy to handle in the field, and its knots are, to me, atypically strong.

Here's why I say that: On the very first trout trip I made after spooling my reel with 6-pound (2.7-kg) Yo-Zuri hybrid, I got a ¼-ounce (7-g) inline spinner snagged in some underwater branches. When that has happened to me in the past, I've

worked and pulled and grunted and swore at the snag, my line and my lure until one of them gave way. More often than not, it was the line, which would break at the knot, costing me another lure.

Not this time. Instead, I was able to apply enough pressure to the lure to literally straighten out the bend of one of the treble hook points, freeing the lure. At the time, I thought that was an aberration; I had just been lucky. But I've done it again three more times since. In fact, I have not lost a snagged lure due to my line breaking since switching to the hybrid. It's amazing, just like most of the other light lines available today.

Interestingly, there don't seem to be as many choices in hybrid lines as there are in pure fluorocarbons. The only one I've been able to track down, beyond Yo-Zuri's, is P-Line's Floroclear, which is a coated line like the one I've had such good luck with. If a hybrid sounds like something you'd like to try, these two appear to be your most likely choices.

Superline

The past decade also has seen development of superlines, most of them braids, that offer significantly increased strength with much smaller diameters. Some of the earliest versions delivered strength equivalent to 40-pound (18-kg) mono, but at the diameter of 10-pound (4.5-kg) mono. Spiderwire was the brand that got lots of attention during the early years of superline because of its performance and, frankly, its marketing plan. This product brought fishing line into a spotlight of sorts, garnering more attention than any line has in years.

Today, Spiderwire is one of several brands of superline that are widely available. Some of the others include Berkley's Ironsilk and FireLine, PowerPro micro-filament line, Tuf-Line and P-Line Spectrex IV. (As is the case in other gear descriptions, this list is not meant to be all-inclusive.)

I recommend that you consider one of them if you are assembling an ultralight rig specifically and exclusively for pike and muskies. It definitely would be worth the investment because the braids have virtually no stretch, which means all of your hook-setting power gets transmitted to the hook—and that's a really good thing when trying to keep a tough-mouthed-and-toothy predator on the end of your line.

Braids also provide superior abrasion resistance. Pike and muskies get away more often simply by wearing out your line than do any other species of fish covered in this book. Especially when you switch to an ultralight approach; that's an important consideration.

It's actually harder to find "cheap" fishing line these days than it is to pick one that will work well for you when applying the techniques presented here. Go with brands you've used and had good luck with in the past; and definitely try a fluorocarbon or hybrid line because they will amaze you with their strength in even the lightest of weights.

I will talk more later about confidence as it relates to equipment. Today's fishing lines inspire more confidence in the ultralight approach for me than ever before. I no longer worry about whether my light line has enough strength to hold up. I know it will.

Fly Fishing Tackle

Here's an angling challenge where some of the rules can change—if you want them to. For example, it is possible to fish dry flies successfully on moving water—even making casts of 50 feet (15 m) and longer—using rods less than 6 feet (1.8 m) long!

When fishing dry flies, going ultralight involves the challenge of using the shortest rods I can find. Later you'll learn that it is not only possible, but not all that tough, to make casts of 50 feet and longer on good-size trout streams using rods less than 6 feet long.

When it comes to fishing subsurface (wet flies, nymphs and the like), I stay with longer rods because using them improves my ability to detect and react to underwater strikes. But I will lighten up, using a 3-weight outfit where other anglers use a 5 or 6.

And that brings me to a brief explanation for readers who are new to fly fishing and some of its terms—like the weighting system used for rods and lines.

Rods and Lines

Fly fishing is different than any other kind of angling because the line you use is the single most important weight additive you have. Lines are designed and built to weigh different amounts and, as such, fit into one of the weight classes used in the industry.

The higher the weight number, the more stout the line and rod. Going ultralight, then, means using the lowest number you can while still having appropriate balance in your fishing gear.

These days, you can find lines and rods that go all the way down to 0-weight, which is lighter than I could even imagine a few years ago. As a frame of reference, consider that the "average" trout outfit is going to be a 5-weight or, on larger western waters, a 6. Bass outfits usually start at 8-weight. Tarpon and other saltwater species usually have anglers using 10-, 11- or even 12-weight rigs.

Remember that the general concept here is that you don't have to go absolutely as light as possible to still be ultralight fishing, and that it's possible to increase your chances with an approach that is ultralight but a little more conservative when compared to the extremes.

The lightest fly fishing outfit I own is a 2-weight. The lightest I use for subsurface fishing is a 3-weight, primarily because there is a wider selection of longer 3-weight outfits available on the market today. For bass, I consider a 5-weight rig to be ultralight, although I use my 3-weight for panfish.

More than thirty years ago, I traded a complete spinning outfit—a classic Garcia-Mitchell 300 reel on a 6-foot (1.8-m) rod—for a flyrod; but not just any flyrod. It was a 5-foot 3-inch (1.6-m) Fenwick fiberglass rod rated for a 5-weight line. Back then, 5 was about as light as things got. But remember, that was before graphite and boron and everything else that has greatly expanded our fly fishing options.

I wanted that rod mostly because I love fishing tiny, native brook trout streams, which are usually choked with shoreline trees and bushes. They make casting difficult, and this little rod, I believed, would help. It did, but it didn't just work well on the little brookie places I fished. It worked well everywhere, although it demands some line-management skills that longer rods don't.

But for our purposes, consider

St Croix's line of Legend Ultra fast-action fly fishing rods carry 2, 3 and 4 line weight models in lengths from 7′ 6″ to 9′.

Nothing beats fighting nice fish on tiny flyrods and ultra-light spinning tackle. It takes some patience because you can't use too much pressure. But, inevitably, your most memorable fishing encounters happen when you fish like this.

it one of two ultralight dry-fly options where shortest is best. Fenwick took that rod out of production in the early 1970s; and, as a result, I hardly used it for years. I sure as heck didn't want to break it when I couldn't replace it. But that's not a worry anymore. Fenwick brought the rod back a few years ago, just like it was back then; 5 feet 3 inches (1.6 m) for a 5-weight line, and fiberglass.

The other shorty option for this scenario excites me even more. You'll find it in the Cabela's fly fishing specialty catalog, a part of the company's

Clear Creek series of rods and combos. This one is a 5-footer (1.5 m), for a 2-weight line. It doesn't get any better than that if you want to add challenge to your dry-fly outings. In sheer size and weight, this is the most ultralight of all.

That being said, I go on record again as saying that I prefer fast actions in my rods, including flyrods. Many manu-facturers offer fast-action rods, but few offer them extremely light or short. One of the best combinations I've found is longer than I like for my ultra-light fly fishing, at 6½ feet

Orvis 8' 6", 5-wt. Streamline rod

Sage's line of extra-light fly fishing rods in the TXL series come in line weights of 00 to 4 and lengths from 7' to 7' 10".

(1.98 m). But it's a 2-weight, and part of the FT series of fast-action rods, also a Cabela's house brand. Fishing it is effortless, as is the case with every fast-action rod I've ever used—fly fishing or spinning.

You'll find similar options from Orvis (which makes the 0-weight lines and rods mentioned earlier), G.Loomis, St. Croix, Fenwick, Redington, Sage and others. These, for the most part, are premium brands and carry higher price tags. Nothing wrong with that; just be warned.

In general, however, you're going to have to go up to a 3-weight to start really seeing a good number of choices. Going to 4 will give you even more, but I start to lose interest when the number gets that high. That's not a whole lot lighter than the 5-weight outfits that have become pretty much rule-of-thumb routine for trout.

I really believe you're better off with longer rods for fishing wets like nymphs, primarily due to their improved strike-detection capabilities. My everyday ultralight outfit is an 8 1/2-foot (2.6-m) 3-weight, and I've even added intermediate and sink-tip lines to this combo. As a result, I can fish flies on, in or just below the surface, or even deeper. A 3-weight is about as light as you can go to find significant line options.

That 3-weight outfit of mine is just right for ultralight pan-fishing because you can take those scrappy warmwater fighters on flies of the average sizes and weights you'd find on just about any trout stream. It will even handle slightly heavier topwater bugs, but not those intended specifically for bass.

For them, I go up to a 5-weight outfit, which is as significantly lighter for bass fishing as a 2-weight is for trout fishing. Yes, there is some difficulty associated with casting fairly large, bulky deer-hair bugs on this light of a rig. But you can do it with some practice, and the payoff comes the first time you hook a 3-pounder (1.4 kg)—or larger—on that fly. What a fight!

Regardless of the size or whether you want to go ultralight for trout, bass or panfish, stick with a floating line if you only can afford—or want to own—one. They are the most versatile, and will permit you to fish just about any kind of fly you want, in just about any depth.

Without question, there are situations where intermediate and/or sink-tip or sinking lines will be better choices. Get them if you can afford them. Just know that the 3-weight outfit I own is the only one for which I have more than just a floating line. And for the record, my fly fishing arsenal includes outfits of 2-, 3-, 5-, 6-, 7- and 8-weights.

Reels

I haven't said much about fly reels yet. There are those who will tell you that they serve little more than as line holders.

I believe it's best to invest the majority of your money in the best rod you can for the kind of fishing you'll do. All you really need is a standard reel, with the most basic of drag systems and a spool large enough to hold your line, and maybe some backing. And you don't have to spend a ton of money to get one.

There are those who believe fly fishing involves—and must inherently include—some kind of mystique perceived from ownership of the best of everything on the market. I disagree. I believe it's all about the challenge of going as light as you can in every situation, and the tackle mentioned here will help you achieve that.

Today's ultralight tackle is much more rugged than you might think. Landing fish on the tiniest of gear is a challenge, but it's more possible than it's ever been because manufacturers are making their UL gear tough and durable.

TACKLE: WHAT YOU NEED TO SUCCEED

Chapter 2

Lures—There Are More Than You Think!

Some anglers view the concept of fishing with ultralight tackle and lures as a very specialized brand of fishing best left to those who don't care whether they actually ever land the fish they hook. Some feel it's for those who crave "fishing on the edge."

Neither could be further from the truth. If this kind of angling really is so specialized, then why are so many different baits available that fit this book's description of ultralight? There are dozens and dozens of them, and they all catch fish.

This book is intended to help you catch more and bigger fish, more often, on lures no heavier than 1/4 ounce (7 g), using rods, reels and lines balanced to handle baits of that size. (Chapter 6 on pike and muskies delves into heavier tackle and baits.)

In this chapter, we'll look at ultralight lures you can use, day in and day out, to make your fishing more enjoyable and more productive. Without a doubt, those who use ultralight tackle and baits on a regular basis already know that's what happens when you lay down your heavier gear. And there's no reason you can't get in on the action.

I've been a fan of the ultralight approach since I first picked up a fishing rod more than thirty-five years ago. At the time, I was so young and inexperienced that most of the "regular size" tackle seemed awkward and heavy to me. Most youngsters and many women naturally lean toward gear that is comfortable in their hands, and the ultralight version of more popular rods, reels and lures certainly are the right size and heft.

The shame of it is that those who help us learn about fishing along the way seem to forget the pure joy and undeniable appeal of ultralight fishing. It seems a traditional rite of passage to "graduate" from the

small stuff to heavier tackle. As a result, many of us forget about what got us hooked on fishing in the first place—the challenge of fooling, hooking, playing and landing fish using gear and baits that, frankly, give our quarry a real, fighting chance.

Oh, sure. In "trout country," you find lots of retail space in tackle shops and big stores that sell sporting goods devoted to UL fishing tackle and baits. Or, you find special sections intended to draw attention from crappie anglers down South and perch fans up North.

Following is a look at the huge number of choices you have when it comes to filling your tackle box with baits that will make ultralight fishing your "go-to" approach, and not just something you choose every now and then because it sounds like it might be fun.

Well, it is fun. And a big part of that fun involves the knowledge that you can fish for any species on any kind of water at any time of the year using baits no heavier than 1/4 ounce (7 g).

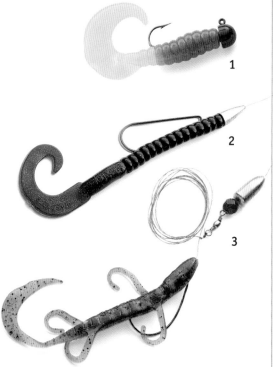

Some plastic baits by Yum: 1) Crawbug, 2) Mega Tube, 3) Walleye Grub, 4) Wooly Curltail, and 5) G-Shad.

A Berkley Power Grub on a mushroom-head jig (1), a Berkley Power Worm rigged Texas-style (2) and a Riverside Floating Air Lizard on a Carolina rig (3).

Soft Plastics

Although the variety and selection of ultralight crankbaits has exploded in the past fifteen-or-so years, soft plastics still provide the widest available selection of lure combinations for ultralight fishing.

All you have to do to lighten up a soft-plastic offering is to change the weight of your jig head, or of the sinker you're using with a Carolina or Texas rig. You have to move up to the largest, longest and bulkiest bass baits you can buy to get into plastic jig, worm and/or grub bodies that, alone, approach 1/4 ounce (7 g).

The Natural Look

These days, it's a good bet that most of the freshwater anglers you know relate ultralight soft plastics either to scrappy little panfish or the concept of "finesse fishing" for bass. What a shame that is.

This isn't really finesse fishing. Using these baits with lighter weights actually is natural fishing; that is, giving the bait you're fishing a more natural look and action in the water.

If you don't believe that, try this experiment: Fill a sink or bathtub with water. Take two plastic worm or grub bodies of the same size; rig one with a 3/8- or 1/2-ounce (10.6- or 14-g) weight, the other with a 1/8-ounce (3.5-g) weight. Then, simply drop them into the water together and watch what happens.

The heavier bait sinks to the bottom much more quickly, which also is much less natural. The lighter bait is going to take longer to settle and, even though the difference is fairly slight, you'll likely notice more natural-looking action in the lighter offering. It might flutter a little as it falls; and if you used a curly-tail worm or grub, that tail certainly will have a more appealing look than one rushing to the bottom behind the much heavier weight.

Remember, day in and day out, fish feed a lot more on healthy, non-injured forage than they do on wounded, dying or dead ones. And that fact absolutely plays into your hands when using ultralight soft plastics. The reason is simple: The lack of weight gives you the ability to make your offering look healthy and natural—like it's just another easy meal going about its business, not really aware of the predator waiting in ambush nearby.

Gamefish are predators, and their normal behavior is to ambush and pick off unsuspecting baitfish, bugs, crawdads and insect larvae under the surface, most often along the bottom. Years of ultralight fishing has made it clear to me that giving those predators a lure that closely resembles what they feed on most often produces more strikes, more often.

You can do that with a variety of soft plastics, using no more than 1/8-ounce (3.5-g) weights. And you can further fine-tune the look, feel and appeal of your lure by playing with line size. Even at the lightest end of the spectrum, fishing line diameter increases as you go heavier; and increased line diameter means more resistance to water.

The same plastic worm

fished on 4-pound (1.8-kg) line using a 1/8-ounce (3.5-g) sinker is going to act differently on your retrieve than if you fish it using a 1/16-ounce (1.7-g) weight on 6-pound (2.7-kg) line. The latter will sink more slowly and look more like a real baitfish because of the lighter weight and increased line diameter. You're likely thinking that the difference can't be enough to be really noticed. Maybe you won't notice it, but fish will.

A Few Options

When it comes to plastics, there are only a handful of lures you need to have in your ultralight arsenal. They include 4- to 6-inch (10- to 15-cm) plastic worms—some straight, others with twister or curly tails; 3- to 4-inch (7.6- to 10-cm) grubs with curly tails; tube baits from the tiniest, for panfish, up to 3 to 4 inches in length; 4-inch "creature" baits like the venerable Hula Grub; and plastic crawdads up to 4 inches.

My rule of thumb concerning when to fish which ultralight soft plastic is simple: I let the structure dictate my choice. Regardless of the species I'm after on a given outing, I opt for the curly-tail grubs or the crawdads on streams. In general, the more rocky the bottom, the more likely I am to use the crawdad. You'll find this kind of structure most prevalent on colder streams that are home primarily to trout and/or smallmouth bass.

On more warmwater streams, you often encounter softer bottoms (the kind a big guy like me will sink deep into when trying to wade). These flows often feature old trees and stumps

Figuring Out Structure

Let's say I'm on the lake, and my first stop is along a stretch of steep shore that drops quickly into 8 to 10 feet (2.4 to 3 m) of water. This is perfect for a plastic worm. I cast it out and, keeping slack line to a minimum, let it freefall to the bottom. When using ultralight tackle and weight, that fall is going to be fairly slow, which is going to keep my lure in the strike zone a lot longer. Any fish relating to the drop will have a chance to see and react to this lure, which appears to be tumbling aimlessly toward the bottom—no doubt in slow motion when compared to the much heavier rigs many anglers use.

At the far end of the drop is a long flat with a sandy bottom and some old stumps here and there. This will be a good place to use the tube bait. I cast it as far as I can; usually I'm in a boat, and will position it so that my longest-possible cast will drop the lure a few inches from the shore. I let it settle for a few seconds, then begin a slow, steady retrieve—an attempt to mimic a baitfish going about its normal routine.

As I approach a point at the far end of the flat, I see a nice weedline up ahead. One of the best ways to fish that kind of structure is to position the boat so you can cast parallel to and just along the outside edge of the weeds, then swim a tube or grub along it.

I round the point to see that I've got 100 yards (91 m) or more of rocky bank. Time for that plastic crawdad or creature, which also presents the look of a crawdad. I cast up to the shore and, as soon as the bait settles, begin to crawl it deliberately over, around and through the rocks. It's the perfect choice for this kind of structure because real crawdads thrive in it, and fish know that. They also love crawdads when they can get them, so I can expect some action from whatever predators are nearby.

along the bottoms, and they offer most of the fish-holding structure. Here, the grubs are better choices because you can crawl them along the bottom or swim them like a baitfish.

No matter the size, when I fish lakes, every soft plastic in my tackle box is a possibility, regardless of whether I'm after crappies, bass, big sunfish, perch or, in cold impoundments, trout. Usually, I have two or three rods rigged and ready; one has a worm, another a tube bait or grub. And if there is plenty of rocky structure to fish, I have a crawdad or creature-style bait on the third. This most often is rigged with a stand-up, mushroom-style jig head because I want the bait to have that crawdad-defensive "stance" when it settles to the bottom.

Kalin Bleepin' Lizard on a G. Mahs Stand-Up Jig

Spinners

What's the first thing that comes into your mind when you hear the words "ultralight spinner?"

Bet it was Mepps or Panther Martin or Rooster Tail. Without question, your immediate mental image was that of one of these lures, or another just like them—an inline spinner that many anglers generally think of only when their quarry is trout. Excuse the pun, but those anglers are really missing the boat when it comes to ultralight spinners. Remember, the weight limit here is 1/4 ounce (7 g).

Today, virtually every maker of the popular safety-pin-style spinnerbait makes at least one model as light as 1/4 ounce. Some are even making smaller versions and marketing them to crappie and panfish anglers.

During the six years that I lived in the Missouri Ozarks, I was fortunate to meet and fish bass tournaments with Steve Holland, who was born and raised on the Missouri shores of Bull Shoals Reservoir and who is as good a bass angler as you'll

ever meet. Holland and I were fortunate enough to cash more than a few checks from tournaments we entered, including winners' shares of payouts.

We caught plenty of keepers on Table Rock Lake and Bull Shoals using spinnerbaits. I never used one weighing more than 1/4 ounce, and Holland rarely did. Day in and day out, bass hit my ultralight spinnerbait with reckless abandon, providing me with the most enjoyable bass action I've ever experienced.

I quickly learned that light spinnerbaits catch tournament-winning stringers. You need them in your arsenal. But not just those 1/4-ounce safety-pin-style baits. You need some of the more traditional UL spinners, too. Take your pick; they all catch fish. Which brand you use will get down to personal taste and the confidence you have in a given brand or style.

Over the years, I've caught fish on practically every spinner on the market. That being said, I do have a favorite style of inline spinner—one that seems to boat or bring to shore more fish than any of the others.

That style is the one where

Booyah Pond Magic, 3/16 oz.

Terminator Wee Tiny-T, 1/16 oz.

Blue Fox Jig 'n Spin, 1/16 oz.

the wire "core" of the lure runs through the spinner blade. Probably the two most well known brands featuring this construction are Panther Martins and the Vibric series from Rooster Tail. You'll find more of these spinners in my boxes than any others—but not necessarily because they catch more fish than any other spinner out there. Instead, it's because I have more confidence in them.

I have the Panther Martin/ Vibric style in sizes from 1/16 to 1/4 ounce (1.7 to 7 g). That black-body/gold-blade model is my personal bread and butter. My closest friend and longtime trout-fishing partner, Jim Galusky, swears just as passionately by either silver or gold lures—bodies and blades—with feather dressings on the treble hooks.

Lure makers, however, don't offer so many color combinations just to hook fishermen. There definitely are times when you have to switch colors to get a strike.

For that reason, my spinner boxes include some other shades beyond the tried-and-true black and gold. I've got some silver and gold, fly-

dressed models, too; and also some bright, almost-fluorescent colors for those days when the skies are dark and the water is off-color.

When it comes to the safety-pin-style spinners, you'll find white and chartreuse models, all in 1/4-ounce weights. And all of them feature tandem willow-leaf blades. I'm sure this goes back to the personal-confidence factor, but these baits have fooled more bass for me than any other size, style or color of spinnerbait I've ever used.

And your spinner box won't be complete without some of those smaller safety-pin baits, which work on everything from little sunfish to big largemouth bass. Probably the oldest of these is the Johnson Beetle Spin; it's been around so long because it works. I fish these in 1/8-ounce (3.5-g) exclusively, and carry them with white, chartreuse and yellow plastic bodies.

What you'll find if you really start looking is that there are more ultralight spinners on the market today than you probably every realized. And they'll catch fish for you in a wide variety of situations.

Rooster Tail Vibric, 1/8 oz.

Panther Martin, 1/8 oz.

Mepps Black Fury, 1/8 oz.

Blue Fox Classic Vibrax, 1/8 oz.

Confidence is the Key

On one recent chilly, overcast late-spring day, I found myself trout fishing on a small lake that was stocked with nice rainbow trout. Just a few yards down the bank from me was another angler fishing a different kind of spinner from mine.

I had a Panther Martin tied on—black body, bare treble hook, gold blade. He, too, was fishing a black spinner with a gold blade and a bare treble, but his was a regular Rooster Tail.

I caught and released a nice, chunky rainbow a few minutes before he arrived, but my succeeding casts were fruitless. His lure was plopping down no more than 20 feet (6 m) from mine; and he took a rainbow with his spinner on the third or fourth cast he made.

My lure boxes are full of Vibrics and Panther Martins because I have confidence in them. His likely are just as full of traditional Panther Martins and Mepps because those are the lures he knows will fool the fish he's after.

This isn't about a specific brand of lure but, rather, about the styles and colors that will work for you. Any angler will catch the most fish on the lures he or she has the most confidence in.

Crankbaits

This is going to sound like the start of a cheap mystery novel; you know, "It was a cold, dark night." In this case, it was a dark, rainy Sunday afternoon in late April.

I stood on the bank of southeastern Oklahoma's Glover River, a clean-flowing, medium-size stream that was home to several species of gamefish. I was trying to decide between a 3-inch (7.6-cm) curly-tail grub and an inline spinner when Oklahoma outdoor writer Lyndol Fry approached with something in his hand.

"Here," he said. "Try this." Fry gave me a tiny crankbait that felt almost weightless in my hand. About 2 inches (5 cm) long, it sported a shallow diving lip and struck me as looking more like a real crawdad than any hard-plastic bait should.

"It's a Wee-Craw," Fry said. "The smallmouths in here really seem to like it."

They sure did. But so did some largemouth bass, big sunfish and rock bass. Along one stretch of the Glover, no more than 50 yards (45.5 m) long, I took four different species of fish on the same lure. I'd never done that before, and I was hooked—not only on this Wee-Craw, but on ultralight crankbaits in general.

If a notice arrived in my mailbox today from the fish police advising me that, effective immediately, all anglers had to choose one kind of bait for all of their fishing and use it exclusively from now on, I would choose crankbaits weighing 1/4 ounce (7 g) or less.

Small Crankbaits like this Wee-Craw offer more options than other lures and will take most species of fish. Anglers have the widest variety ever of UL crankbaits to choose from, and they imitate practically every possible natural fish food, from terrestrials to minnows and, of course, crawfish.

It's safe to suggest that this type of lure offers ultralight anglers more options than any other. There are crawdad imitations like the Wee-Craw, baitfish imitations, lipless crankbaits, wigglers, wobblers, even topwater plugs—all of them in ultralight sizes. If you want to change your approach to fishing forever—and if you take nothing else from the pages of this book as a technique you want to try—spend some time fishing ultralight crankbaits. You just won't believe how effective they are until you've seen it for yourself.

To prove the point, I just logged on and did a Web search using the term ultralight crankbaits. The results included more than 1,300 Web pages!

After the success I enjoyed with the Wee-Craw, I wanted to find out whether other little lures actually would catch fish. It didn't take long to learn that the answer was a resounding yes. And from there, my goal has been to add UL crankbaits simply to give myself more options to cover more fish and fishing situations.

I've used the Wee-Craw, made by Rebel, more than any other because, thanks to Lyndol Fry, it was the UL crankbait I started out with. And for the record, I have caught seventeen species of gamefish on that one lure: largemouth, smallmouth, spotted and rock bass; white bass; black and white crappies; bluegills; orange-spotted and green sunfish; rainbow, brook and brown trout; channel and flathead catfish; saugers; and walleyes.

I've also taken some combination of all of those species on literally every UL plug I've ever tried. They've come throughout the fishing season; these baits are not limited in their effectiveness to that time of year when the primary forage in a given body of water is about the same size (as when young bait fish are swimming around in large schools).

And don't think for a minute that these baits are going to catch only small- or average-size fish. My arsenal of UL crankbaits has fooled bass of more than 3 pounds (1.4 kg); slabside crappies over 1 pound (0.45 kg); trout pushing 16 inches (41 cm). These little baits aren't just for little fish.

A Few Options

Here are my thoughts on some of the lures you can pick and choose from to get started with UL plugs.

Make sure you have some Wee-Craws, which Rebel officially calls the 77 series. I use Nos. 7760 and 7734 exclusively. The last two digits of those numbers are keyed to the lures' colors—60 is natural dark

green—with an orange belly; 34
is chartreuse with an orange
belly. I use the former in clear
water, the latter in stained
water and on dark days.

Minnow imitations are myriad
in ultralight sizes these days.
All of the major manufacturers
have at least one model in their
lineup that weighs 1/4 ounce
(7 g) or less.

Among the most well-known
lure makers with UL models are
Rapala (jointed and regular
Shad Rap, and the Countdown
Rapala), Bill Lewis Lures (the
Mini Trap and Tiny Trap versions
of the Rat-L-Trap), Rebel (minnow baits in addition to the
Wee-Craw, and a whole line of
other ultralight plugs), Yo-Zuri
(the 3D Minnow is among several models available in UL
weights), Cotton Cordell (the
Wally Diver) and many others.

When it comes to colors, I
apply the same rule of thumb
with minnow baits as I do the
little crawdad; that is, use
natural shades in clear to
slightly stained water, and on
days with plenty of light. Go
for the brighter hues early and
late in the day, when there's
heavy overcast, or when the
water is dirty. Fire tiger is an
all-around choice in a bright
color pattern, and pretty much
every manufacturer offers its
UL lures in some version of a
fire tiger pattern.

The standard black- or blue-
over-silver and black-over-gold
color patterns also are highly
effective. My experience has
been to use the silver-sided
baits, especially blue-over-silver, when there is plenty of
sunshine. The black-over-gold
pattern works consistently well
in clear to slightly stained
water on cloudy days.

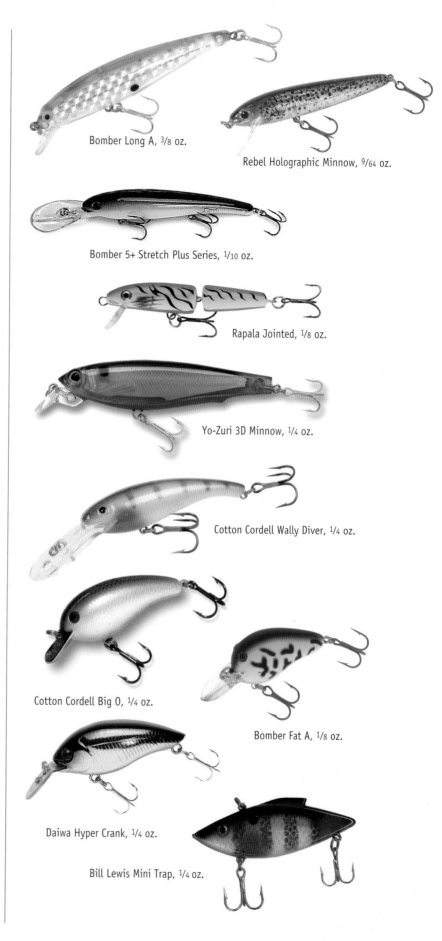

Bomber Long A, 3/8 oz.

Rebel Holographic Minnow, 9/64 oz.

Bomber 5+ Stretch Plus Series, 1/10 oz.

Rapala Jointed, 1/8 oz.

Yo-Zuri 3D Minnow, 1/4 oz.

Cotton Cordell Wally Diver, 1/4 oz.

Cotton Cordell Big O, 1/4 oz.

Bomber Fat A, 1/8 oz.

Daiwa Hyper Crank, 1/4 oz.

Bill Lewis Mini Trap, 1/4 oz.

LURES—THERE ARE MORE THAN YOU THINK!

Water Types

When I fish streams and plan to use ultralight crankbaits, I tend to stick with the crawdad imitations or one of the little Rat-L-Traps because they are consistent producers. I may opt for the crawdad when fishing stretches with plenty of rocks or shoreline weeds.

I switch to the small Rat-L-Trap when I get to deeper pools of water, or when fishing during periods of high water on a given stream because these baits sink. You can get them down to the bottom where the biggest fish in a given pool or deep run often are hiding out. And just as importantly, you can work them along the edges of swifter currents in the high water. Whether it's bass or trout, stream fish use current breaks as holding lies, and a crankbait that you can work effectively along those breaks will take fish consistently.

I also fish the Trap on softer-bottom streams, where the structure is mostly trees and branches deposited by swift, high water. This generally is a kind of fishing area that won't hold many crawdads, so the baitfish imitation makes more sense.

And, finally, when nothing else seems to be working on stream fish, the Trap makes a great bait to rip just under the surface. Admittedly, it's not a natural look, but there are times when fish will strike at a bait zooming past their ambush point.

In lakes of any size, you should choose and fish ultralight crankbaits just as you would their larger, heavier brethren. Use crawdad patterns in rocky cover; minnow imitations there and along most any other kind of structure. Diminutive size and weight does not keep these lures from being any less effective. You should use them the same way as the larger plugs because they work the same way, in the same places, on the same fish.

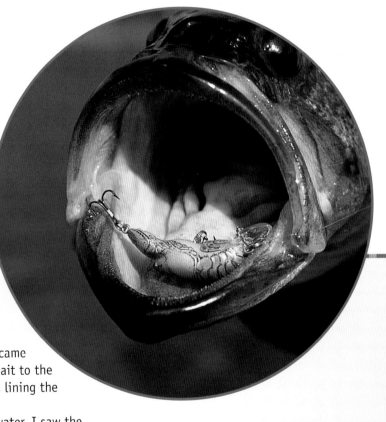

Surprise Hit

One of the most memorable encounters with a stream bass came when I threw a little crawdad bait to the outer edge of a clump of weeds lining the bank of a small pool.

The second my lure hit the water, I saw the tops of the weeds move. I didn't even make three full cranks of the reel handle before a 2-pound (0.9-kg) largemouth smacked the bait hard and jumped clean out of the water. What a fighter, and what a good lesson to learn.

Many anglers, me included, might have passed up the chance to fish these weeds because there were so many other good-looking spots within casting distance. But something told me to make a presentation in that direction; honestly, though, I was expecting a sunfish.

That bass showed me that bigger fish will use little pockets of weeds like this, and they'll hit tiny crankbaits that come meandering nearby.

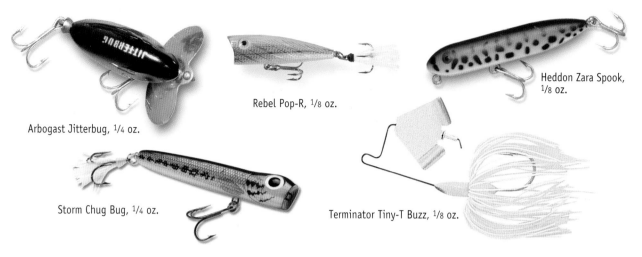

Arbogast Jitterbug, 1/4 oz.

Rebel Pop-R, 1/8 oz.

Heddon Zara Spook, 1/8 oz.

Storm Chug Bug, 1/4 oz.

Terminator Tiny-T Buzz, 1/8 oz.

Topwater Baits

Yes, there are ultralight versions of the most effective topwater lures around. You can and should fish buzzbaits, poppers and walking baits weighing 1/4 ounce (7 g) or less anywhere you'd use their larger counterparts.

Of the three, buzzbaits are liable to fool you because they most resemble their heavier relatives. Blades and skirts are usually the same size, as are the dimensions of the baits. What changes is the amount of weight on the head. This makes UL buzzbaits especially good choices because they present pretty much the same silhouette to the fish that will hit them.

There are no shortage of buzzbait makers. Major mail-order retailers such as Bass Pro Shops and Cabela's offer house brands, and there are other widely distributed brands like Terminator. But if you have a local bait shop or marina close to where you fish, chances are that you'll find a nice selection of locally made buzzers that will fit the bill nicely.

I stick to the same color patterns as my safety-pin-style spinnerbaits—white and char-

treuse—with one exception. Over the years, I've learned that buzzers with black skirts really provide an enticing look in periods of very low light, and after dark.

Poppers and walking baits are usually at least one-third smaller, as ultralights, than "standard" baits of the same design. My experience has been that the downsizing doesn't much affect the kind of attention they attract from the fish.

Among the most popular popping plugs are the Rebel Pop-R and the Storm Chug Bug. The Heddon Zara Spook probably is the most well known walking bait in freshwater fishing history. Arbogast's venerable Jitterbug provides what some might call the best of both styles. It chugs along in the surface film displacing water like a popper. But using a jerky retrieve will make it walk—not exactly like a Zara Spook, but with a very interesting and bite-enticing action.

And here's something you might not think about: Literally any floating minnow bait can be fished as a walking bait—traditional Rapala models, Smithwick Rogues, Storm Thundersticks, Bomber Long As, Bill Lewis Slapsticks. Any

long minnow bait that floats at rest can be walked along the surface, and all of them will catch fish.

Again, don't consider this list all-inclusive. It's not, and not intended to be. A trip down the aisles of your favorite bait shop will reveal many more options for UL fishing on top.

My favorite topwater UL is a popping bait. I generally carry them in natural colors, fire tiger and, when I can find them, clear or transparent shades. The latter, along with the fire tiger, work best for me on overcast days, early in the morning and on the last rays of a setting sun. I usually opt for the natural baitfish colors on bluebird days, or when there are schools of baitfish active on or very near the surface.

And here's a tip that could improve your success when using either poppers or hard, walking baits: Instead of just tying them straight to your line, use either a snap swivel or a plain metal snap. When you attach the eye of your lure to one of these, you'll gain more erratic action, and the bait won't be so rigid at rest. This is especially important with poppers, between twitches of your rod tip on the retrieve.

Spoons

Yes, there are ultralight spoons; and yes, they catch fish.

My introduction to spoons came more than thirty years ago when, as a young trout fisherman, I stood next to anglers who were taking their limit on a Super Duper—a tiny spoon-style lure that actually looks like a little tuning fork with a treble hook on the end. I have no idea what trout think it is, but the darned thing catches them even today.

Although there are plenty of spoons on the market from a variety of manufacturers, most of the ultralight models you find come from either Johnson, Dardevle or Mepps. Johnson's well-known Silver Minnow is available as small as 1/24 ounce (1.2 g), and it's a good bet when you want to try something a little different to imitate a baitfish.

Dardevle offers spoons lighter than 1/4 ounce (7 g) in a rainbow of colors, and Mepps Cyclops spoons are available in UL sizes in gold, silver and black. They are interesting twists on traditional spoons in that you can rig them with a small, plastic curly-tail grub that gives them a totally different look and action.

Because the Silver Minnow is built using a single weedless hook, you also can rig it with a trailer. My experience in the ultralight sizes, however, has been that plain works best because you can swim the lure over, through and around anything and—especially in silver—get a baitfish look to your presentation.

Dardevles are rigged with treble hooks except for their very smallest models, which come with a twin-point hook. That lure has taken plenty of trout for me over the years, and all of these spoons are really easy to fish.

I swim them, just as I would a crankbait. Their appeal is that they move differently than a crankbait and offer a slightly different look in the water—one that fish definitely move in on and strike.

That Cyclops, with the curly-tail grub attached, also gives you a fairly weedless and snag-free lure that can be crawled along the bottom to mimic a crawdad.

As mentioned, I prefer the Silver Minnow in silver, which is good because it's the shade you're going to find in ultralight sizes. Most of my Cyclops spoons are gold or black; and when I use a plastic trailer, it's black.

Dardevles are where my color palate expands significantly because, well, it can! UL Dardevles come in all colors, including the most traditional of all—red and white. I have some of those, and also some blue and silver ones. Fire tiger looks good and works well, as does the frog pattern. They're not exactly crankbaits, but these spoons are just as effective in ultralight sizes.

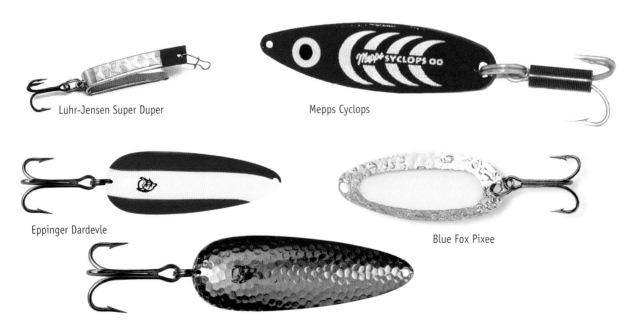

Luhr-Jensen Super Duper

Mepps Cyclops

Eppinger Dardevle

Blue Fox Pixee

Chapter 3

Water—Read It and See Fish

Most of this book deals with the rods, reels, lines, baits and techniques that will help you catch plenty of fish—and big fish—on ultralight tackle. There's a lot to talk about with all of those elements; but they're not the only things that affect your ability to catch more fish more often.

Anglers who enjoy the most consistent success are those who know what they see when they look at the water. They've learned the subtle keys that help them figure out exactly where the fish are and, as a result, exactly how they need to fish a certain spot to have the best chance for a hookup.

Flyrodders and those who mostly fish streams call it "reading the water." But it doesn't just apply to fishing places where the water flows. Everywhere fish live, there are keys you can use to help figure out exactly where they might be, and how best to present your bait or lure to coax a strike. And once you get used to the exercise, you will improve your ability to catch fish on ultralight tackle every time you hit the water—even if it's unknown to you.

To illustrate, let me tell you about the one-eyed largemouth I caught several years ago on Lake Olathe, the community impoundment I fished often when I lived and worked in the Kansas City suburbs. If there ever was a true on-the-water classroom for an angler, Lake Olathe was such a place for me.

One midsummer evening, one of my fishing partners, Jim Givens, and I had the boat out fishing through our usual spots in search of bass and whatever else might come along. The lake's main feeder creek flowed into its southeast corner, the narrow channel slowly opening into a nice little bay that eventually widened even more into the main lake.

At one spot, a little finger of land jutted out, creating a tiny pocket on its back side where Givens and I always had done pretty well. We were heading there that evening when, for some reason, I decided to cast my ultralight crankbait just beyond the tip of that little weed-covered point. The lure splashed down about a yard (meter) from the weeds, on their far side. I remember seeing a couple of those weeds move just before a fish absolutely annihilated my lure.

I reeled the fish toward the boat, and it jumped once or twice, putting up a nice fight. As it drew near the aluminum hull, Givens leaned over from the captain's chair and lipped the foot-long bass. "Hey!" he said almost immediately. "Look at this. This fish only has one eye." I expected to see an empty eye socket, suggesting foul hooking from an earlier encounter with a fisherman or, possibly, unfortunate rough treatment by another angler.

Fish favor certain "spots" to wait for prey—find these locations in a body of water and they will produce fish time after time. When you take a good fish from one of these spots, another one replaces it. The best ambush locations are consistent producers.

hidden out and still been an effective predator. Facing the main lake with its snout pointing west/southwest, this bass had the right side of its body tucked tightly into the weeds. It didn't have to worry about predation from that side—which it couldn't see anyway—because of the thick cover and shallow water. This bass was less than 3 feet (0.9 m) from dry land, but its left side, which provided its only vision, faced the open water and could spy anything coming by. Its position was such that the routinely prevailing breezes, which came out of the west or south, would help move easy meals into range.

Talk about resourceful! Although small, this bass remains one of the most memorable—and valuable—I've ever caught. Just a few weeks later, I began to understand that much more fully.

Fishing with another buddy on Lake Olathe, we found ourselves within casting range of that very spot. "Throw your worm just beyond that little weedy tip, Harry," I suggested. "There ought to be a fish there." He did, and was rewarded by the strike of a bass weighing more than 5 pounds (2.25 kg), a true Lake Olathe trophy. It was during that encounter that I began to understand the dynamics of reading every water I fished, learning how and why fish use the spots they do.

You can do the same thing, and I hope that what follows will help you become good at it more quickly than I did. Just as using the right ultralight baits and fishing rigs, reading the water can make you a much better angler.

Not this time; this bass was different. There was nothing on the right side of its nose to suggest that it ever had an eye there. Smooth, emerald-green skin shimmered under its scales in the warm rays of a setting sun. The left side of its face looked perfectly normal. I believe this bass hatched without a right eye, and it learned to adapt well enough to grow to adult size in this lake, where large bass were few and far between.

Neither one of us had a camera, but my mental image of that bass—and the lesson it taught me—remains as vivid today as it was when it happened. It was this bass that really made me sensitive to the concept of reading still water and learning how fish use their hiding places.

The spot where that fish was hiding—or one just like it—is the only place it could have

Lakes and Ponds

Two factors made Lake Olathe such an outstanding classroom for my education in reading still water. First, it was relatively small—pushing 300 acres (120 hectares) when it was plum full after early spring rains. Second, it was close. If I got home from work in the evening and decided I wanted to go fishing, I literally could have the boat launched, the truck parked and be making casts less than twenty minutes later.

This lake also features a dynamic variety of cover types, especially for one its size: brush piles, weedlines, flats, bluffs, rocky banks, flooded trees. It always offered a lesson or two on every visit.

Fish Hideouts

One lesson I learned was that fish use the same ambush spots all the time. If you catch and remove a fish from a spot, another will take its place. So, you can predict with accuracy those spots on your favorite lake that will be consistent fish producers.

Don't mistake this to suggest that you'll take a nice bass or crappie or trout from a given spot every single time you visit. Too many variables out of your control make that impossible. What I'm saying is that over the long term, those places where you've caught fish in the past will hold them again and again.

Next, to increase your knowledge even more, you need to figure out why. I'll use the little weedy point mentioned earlier as an example: It not only provides predators with good cover, but its orientation is such that,

Look for a variety of cover types like flooded trees, weedlines and dense weed beds or rocky banks. Then locate areas within the cover that hold fish. Usually they will be the hideouts of fish more often than not.

when fish move into ambush position, they are facing prevailing breezes most of the time. They are going to have meals blown right at them by wave action every time the wind gets stiff enough. And there's deeper water nearby. Fish lay on the south side of that point in ambush. On its north side, the bottom drops quickly to about 15 feet (4.5 m). If fish need to move deep, they can do so without going very far.

That's as close to the perfect big-fish hideout as I've ever seen on a lake. And I bet that if you take some time to think about all the elements that make up a certain consistent-fish-holding spot that you know of, you'll come up with a similar mix of good reasons for it.

Finally, you can take everything you learn to yet another level by visiting unknown waters and trying to determine the most likely places to fish.

Natural elements don't change from lake to pond to reservoir. Fish are going to use certain spots on every lake, regardless of its size, for one or more of the reasons mentioned just now—cover, physical orientation, proximity to deep water, or all of them.

It's a good bet that many of you reading this book make trips to exotic fishing destinations. Maybe you go to Canada after smallmouth bass, or pike and muskie. Maybe you head to Texas or Florida for lunker largemouths.

If you can grasp the concepts in this section through use on waters near home that are already familiar to you, you're going to improve your odds for success on foreign impoundments—regardless of their size—because you'll have a much better idea of the kinds of spots you ought to be fishing.

So as you fish your favorite lakes this season and in the future, begin to learn which places always seem to hold fish; then, begin to figure out why that's the case. Doing that will help you find more fish more often, and catch them more consistently.

Hidden Structure

There's also another kind of fish-holding element on many lakes around the country that will pay huge dividends for you—if and when you can learn about them. I was fortunate to have another angler show me one of these hidden structure areas at the back of a large cove on Missouri's Table Rock Lake.

"You are not going to believe this place," Penny Berryman told me as we headed out one evening. "It's the kind of spot that you have to know is there because you'd never suspect it otherwise."

She was right. On the lake's detailed topographic map, all you see is a fairly flat point that spreads out from the shore about 150 yards (136 m). The water never gets more than about 10 feet (3 m) deep, until it drops suddenly into 30 feet (9 m) of water. When I got home from fishing that night and looked at the map, I thought that if I was depending on the map and figuring out where to fish, I would have concentrated on that break.

And that would have been a mistake because the real fish magnet at this spot was 60 to 70 yards (55 to 64 m) closer to the shore. On one side of that point, there's an underwater area maybe 15 to 20 yards (14 to 18 m) in diameter that features a hefty rock pile. Smallmouth bass must live on it because Berryman and I each caught bronzebacks off of it that evening, and I never failed to at least get one bite on every single stop there afterward—and I'm talking about a three-year period!

The first time back after Berryman showed me the spot, I trolled slowly back and forth over it paying attention to the fish finder. Sure enough, you could see the rock pile on the display very distinctly. But most anglers simply wouldn't ever think to look for structure like that in that location.

Remember those exotic trips mentioned earlier? Often, you don't have the luxury of having your own boat and electronics; but just as often, that's because you'll be fishing with a guide using his or an outfitter's boat and electronics. Your structure knowledge can still make an impact.

Say, for example, that you've discovered a flooded rock pile on your favorite bass lake like the one Berryman showed me on Table Rock. Only in your case, that rock pile sits a few yards (meters) off the end of a main-lake point. You now have two kinds of potential hotspots to inquire about.

Ask your guide or outfitter whether they know of little areas like the one on Table Rock or the one you discovered on your own lake. Then, check them out. There's a good chance you'll catch fish off them.

What's the point, you ask? Simple. Even on your favorite lake, reading the water also should mean taking the time to look for those hidden hotspots that only your fish finder will show you. It might even mean spending a day on the water doing a whole lot more searching than fishing. But believe this: It will pay off for you in the long run.

Global Positioning System

Many of today's fish finders include a GPS function. If yours does, begin marking those spots to make them much easier to pinpoint in the future. If you don't have a GPS unit, give serious thought to investing in a handheld model. Their retail prices continue to drop, and they can pay huge dividends for you when it comes to finding your favorite lake's hidden hotspots and returning to them quickly on every visit.

During periods of low water, you can use a handheld GPS to precisely mark the location of spots that hold fish when they're submerged. This is an unbeatable way to increase your odds of catching fish on every trip.

Although this doesn't have much to do with reading water, I think it's important to note that GPS also provides the ability to visit and fish the largest of strange waters without worrying about getting lost. Beginning with your launch point, you simply use the unit to mark spots along your outing; you can then retrace your steps to find your way home. It's a great feature that many anglers don't even think about.

Of course, you'd never need GPS on a pond. The sad mistake that some anglers make is believing they don't need to read the water on them, either, because they're so small.

I know of a pond I fished regularly, only 2 acres (0.8 hectare) when full to the brim, that had more underwater secrets than I ever realized. Its owner had built a rock pile in its south end. He'd planted a brush pile in the deepest part of the lake. He'd put rocks at one corner of the earthen dam face, and he built the pond over an underground spring that fed it.

In that one paragraph, you've been given enough information to reduce a 2-acre pond to four much smaller hotspots for the fish. Every pond you can think of has some kind of fish-holding elements that, when you know of them, will help you get on fish in a hurry and catch them every time you visit.

Fishing small ponds becomes a really fun adventure when you read them to learn their secrets. From then on, you can concentrate your efforts on the best places. Then, after you've taken fish from there—or if they seem like they're off the bite the day you visit—you can spend some time fishing the rest of the pothole thoroughly to pick up any other fish that might be on the move and ready to bite.

Sunlight

There's one other element to reading lakes and ponds that can help you catch fish more consistently. That is to begin noting how the sun's movement through the sky impacts those spots you like to fish the most. Which places stay in the shade the longest in the morning? Which places get back in the shade first as the afternoon wears on? Learning this will help you immensely.

If you're planning a sunrise visit, fish the spots first that the sun will hit first. Once the warming morning rays start bathing the surface in light, fish are going to either become less aggressive, or they'll move to deeper water—or both. Plan your day so that you fish as many spots as possible before the morning light hits them. This will put the odds in your favor.

If you can't get out till after work, think about it the opposite way. Which places have been in the shade the longest? Fish them first, and let the sun move off the rest of your consistent producers before you move to them.

Early in the year, this isn't something to be too worried about because while water temperatures are still low, fish actually respond positively to sun on the water. But from the end of the spawn through Labor Day (maybe a little later, depending on where you live), reading the water for sunlight is an important factor.

During hot weather, concentrate on shady areas. Especially during the middle of the day, fish will locate to structure in these spots, and they will tend to be more aggressive than if they were in bright sunlight.

Streams

There probably has been as much written about reading streams as there has about any other element of fishing moving water. But when you're using ultralight tackle and baits, there are some elements of this process that will be more important than ever to you.

Among them is the fact that, just as in lakes and ponds, good fish-holding spots will always be good fish-holding spots. If you take a nice trout or rock bass from a given place, you can pretty much expect a fish to be there every time you visit if conditions are similar.

That last part is very important because some anglers don't seem to think much about how changes in current strength and water level affect riffles and pools on a stream. Fish spread out when the water is up, and you face a bigger challenge in finding and catching them.

Current Strength

If you've done any stream fishing at all, or if you've read other books or seen TV fishing shows taped on flowing water, you know that current breaks are extremely important to the fish living in a given stream. How many times have you focused on getting your fly or lure to drift just on the edge of the current, knowing that any fish in the spot were going to be lying in ambush just out of the main current?

With that in mind, take one of your favorite riffles, and imagine a heavy rain raising its level by a foot or more. What happens? Most often, you arrive to find several current breaks, the increased water changing the

High-Water Mishap

My trout-fishing partner, Jim Galusky, took me to a tiny stream in western Maryland where, on a trip less than 10 days earlier, he'd caught and released a native brook trout more than a foot (30.5 cm) long. He knows that the biggest native I've ever caught measured 11½ inches (29 cm), and that my personal "Moby Dick" is a native 12 inches or longer.

"It's up," he said, as we parked along the stream. "All that rain from the other day raised it pretty good." He led me to a tiny spot of calm water between low waterfalls created by tree trunks lying across the creek.

"See where the water's bubbling over that first tree?" he asked. "That's where it hit."

Focusing on the spot, I hurried to the edge of the stream without thinking about the impact of the water being almost a foot higher than it was when Galusky was last here.

"Oh, no!" I shrieked. "I just blew it."

"What happened?" Jim asked. "That big brookie was lying over here in the calm water, and I spooked him when I walked up to the stream. I watched him head right for where you said he hit the other day."

"This water wasn't high like this," he offered. "He was lying right at the base of the main falls."

I cast more than a dozen times in futility. That day's only chance at the trophy I'd been after for decades had been blown in my rush to start fishing without reading the water in front of me.

dynamic of the spot significantly.

Always remember that when this happens, fish are liable to use any or all of those other feeding lanes. If you don't believe it, step into the riffle or pool at its very tail, and pay attention as you slowly move through it. Unless the water is the color of strong coffee with cream, you'll have enough visibility to see the fish that move up toward the head of the run or pool as you spook them. You might even be surprised at how spread out they are.

Water Level

I believe one of the most overlooked elements of reading streams is thinking of them differently during periods of high water. They do become different streams, and you have to fish them differently.

In this case, differently means completely. Don't pass a feeding lane without making a cast or two at or through it. Fish upstream whenever possible, and cover every little current tongue thoroughly. Above all, take your time.

Some readers who are stream veterans may disagree with me, but I take an approach that's just the opposite during the summer and early fall, when water levels generally are at their lowest. Experience has taught me that you most often only get one chance at low-water fish. So, you have to plan your presentation and make the most of it.

Streams are much more dynamic than some anglers ever give them credit for. As a result, many fishermen often blow chances at good fish because they either don't fish thoroughly enough during high water or they don't fish carefully enough during low water.

When you go out West—say, to trout fish some of America's most well known and highly productive waters, like the Yellowstone or Bighorn—don't be intimidated by the size of the rivers. Instead, break them up: You can fit several streams the width of a typical eastern freestone brook into any number of productive stretches you'll encounter on a western river like the Yellowstone. When you encounter larger water like this, take the time to read it in sections that you can reach. Look for the best spots within each section, and fish them. It's a key to success, especially when you're not a regular visitor to the water you're on.

Another complication of sorts you'll encounter on larger water are those sections that are best fished by boat. And they aren't limited just to the good streams in the Rocky Mountains or the Pacific Northwest. Many trout anglers, for example, have heard of that section of Arkansas' White River, below Bull Shoals Reservoir, that is home to some of the largest brown trout you'll find anywhere. Often, this part of the White is fishable only by floating.

When faced with this kind of angling, you can still read the water and locate the most productive spots. Sure, your perspective changes, and often, you'll only get one shot at a great location because you're moving downstream with the current. But the rules of reading water still apply.

Low-Water Tactics

One time, Jim Galusky and I had been on Glady Fork, a medium-size river in Randolph County, West Virginia, whose population of wild and native trout is supplemented with weekly stockings from March through May. That late-June day found the water low, at its normal summer level. Fish were few and far between.

I watched Galusky fish the pool at the base of a low falls for 15 to 20 minutes with no luck. He covered it about as thoroughly as any angler could, with not even a bite. As he moved toward the next inviting spot, I couldn't help but think there just had to be a trout there. But I could only think of one presentation that Galusky hadn't tried.

Moving into position at the top of the little falls, which was created by a tree blown over the creek, I pitched my little crawdad

imitation crankbait to the tail of the pool below. I let the current impart most of the lure's action, and I retrieved it as slowly as possible toward the bubbling water directly below me. I was a split-second from lifting the bait out of the water when a 13-inch (33-cm) rainbow smacked it hard.

That fish literally was lying under the tree, using the calm water behind it and watching for an easy meal to tumble over the falls in front of it. When my lure hit that rush of water, this trout rushed to feed.

The key for me was reading the water. I caught two more trout that same way during this outing, learning a big lesson in the process. I've used the tactic again and again during periods of low water to fool trout that many other anglers undoubtedly walked right by.

Putting It All Together

The whole point of reading water, be it flowing or still, is to think of it as doing the homework you need to pass the test of a fishing trip. Remember that on every kind of water you fish, there are certain places that always hold fish. Your first step to success is to identify as many of them as possible.

Next, take the time to figure out exactly what it is about that spot that makes it such a good ambush point for predatory gamefish. Consider water depth, available cover, how prevailing breezes or, in a stream, current flow impact the spot.

Then, start paying attention to other spots you encounter on a given outing. Measure them against the elements that make your known hotspots so good, and fish those that seem to stack up. If you catch fish from them, note their location and, over time, learn whether they are as consistent as the others you've located.

Every time you do this, you're expanding your ability to fish effectively. You've probably heard the old cliché that you won't catch a fish without having your bait or lure in the water. What I'm suggesting with this information on reading water is that you're going to greatly improve your chances to catch fish by keeping your offering in the known strike zones of given spots as long as possible.

During periods of low, clear (or relatively clear) water on your favorite lakes and ponds, take the time to identify good fish-holding structures that are usually submerged for most of the season. Think about the best presentations to use. Literally make notes if you have to.

Spend some time idling around coves, feeder creeks and other good spots on your favorite impoundments searching out underwater cover that you'd otherwise not know about. If you can, use GPS to pinpoint their locations or, again, make notes on visible landmarks that can help you line up and locate those spots again.

On still water and streams, pay attention to the sun's movement across the sky, and learn how and where it hits some of the spots that are consistent producers for you. During the hottest parts of the season, that knowledge will pay dividends for you as you plan exactly when and how to fish those areas.

On streams, let the creek level be your first stop at reading the water during any given outing. Think through the differences of when the water's high and when it's low.

In either case—regardless of water level, in fact—focus your efforts on those areas of slack or slower water just off the main current. The eddies created by midstream rocks are among the best ambush points of all for resident fish, and don't pass any spot by that offers fish a chance to settle in and wait for an easy meal to drift close by.

If the water is up, think about every possible holding spot before you make a single cast. Then, work your way through a given riffle or pool by fishing those spots you'll have to wade through or walk by to get to other spots. Failing to do this is very likely to cost you fish that you'll spook before you ever get a chance to hook them.

When the water is low and clear, take the time to analyze a given riffle or pool, and decide which specific spots are the most likely to hold fish. Then, determine the presentation that will give you the best single opportunity to fool a fish hiding there.

Regardless of species, stream fish are at their most skittish during these periods of low, clear water. Don't ever plan on getting more than one chance at a given spot, and take the time to make the most of that chance.

Then, before moving on, look closely to see whether there might be a spot that doesn't seem so obvious—like slack water under a tree or rock ledge that creates a waterfall. Pools below these spots often appear empty simply because the fish are hiding where most anglers don't look for them.

Chapter 4

Bass

My legs burned by the time I made my first cast. It was a long kick across this 250-acre (100-hectare) municipal lake in eastern Kansas. I'd seen many boats on it; but mine, I believe, was the first float tube ever to cross the lake.

A beautiful morning greeted me as I eased the tube into the water, climbed in and started kicking my way southwest. It was a little after 8:00, and the still-rising sun was warming the day nicely. I wondered whether the water would feel chilly; it didn't. But some of that undoubtedly had to do with the workout my legs were getting.

As much as I wanted to fish, I couldn't bring myself to hurry. There wasn't another soul on the lake. And although by this time of morning folks were out

and about, this place was located on the west edge of town. It was still quiet; only the birds' songs and the barely audible buzz of a far-off mower mixing with the splashing of my swim fins breaking the surface film now and then.

I kicked for a minute, then drifted for two, drinking in the serenity of the moment. Little did I know how things soon would get so much more exciting.

In my hand was a light-action baitcasting rod with a state-of-the-art, closed-face spincasting reel. It was spooled with 6-pound (2.7-kg) line, and I had a 1/8-ounce (3.5-g) minnow-imitation crankbait tied on.

It was the perfect "hatch-matching" lure for this place, which was full of small baitfish. By now, only a week or so from summer's official arrival, those fish congregated in large schools and shadowed the surface on warm late-spring evenings. Their size matched perfectly the length and contour of the lure I had tied on.

Soon enough, I reached the

southwest corner of the lake, an area mixing rocky shoreline with old trees and brush piles. It was a perfect fish-holding area, and every previous visit had produced either a large-mouth or two, or several nice green sunfish. Bank fishermen also used it frequently, making it about the busiest area of the whole lake.

I cast to a shoreline that saw a lot of fishing pressure, using an ultralight crankbait while fishing from a quiet float tube. I hoped that this approach would attract some interest from fish not used to seeing smaller lures without the nearby shadow of a large boat hull.

It did.

Things didn't start out quickly, however. I actually was becoming a little discouraged after casting to what had always been the most productive parts of the shoreline without even a bump. Now moving east along the lake's south shoreline, I began casting straight ahead of me into open water, probably 20 yards (18 m) from the bank. I knew from experience that the channel

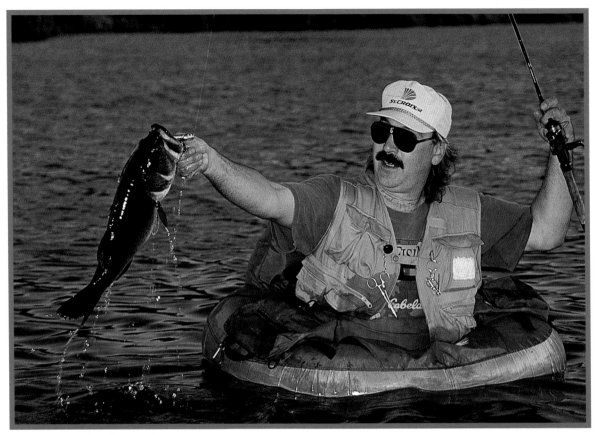

Fishing out of a float tube can give you a real advantage because you can get into casting positions that are impossible from the shore. And tubing is the ultimate in quiet. Big fish won't even know you're around until they bite and you set the hook.

meandered about 12 feet (3.7 m) under me, and that there were the odd tree stumps and old limbs dotting its edges.

After maybe a half-dozen casts over the channel, a 4-pound (1.8-kg) largemouth inhaled the crankbait. But it didn't give its size away—not until it finally saw the tube, with me in it. Then, all hell broke loose!

I laughed out loud at the commotion as the fish spun me round and round; jumped; bulled deep. It was the most exciting fight I've ever had with a bass, all on ultralight tackle.

Things turned comical when I tried to "land" it—that is, to lip it long enough to unhook the bait and release it. We danced in circles for a minute or two because every time I tried to grab the fish, it'd

writhe away and spin me in the tube. Mostly, we turned counterclockwise.

This proved to be a lot more fun than it did frustrating, although I realized after a few 360s that landing this feisty largemouth in the tube, in the water, would be problematic at best. So I kicked over to shore, stood up and took care of business. I also took a few quick photos using my little camera's self-timer.

Now, don't think you have to use a belly boat and little crankbaits to catch bass on ultralight gear. Although it truly is a hoot, it's not the only way to catch big bass on ultralight tackle. In fact, you can take lunkers from the surface all the way to the bottom on a variety of baits. Here's what you need to know.

What Other Fish Tell You

If you're a veteran bass angler who has been using the more traditional sizes and weights of rods, reels, lines and lures, you're going to learn something new right off the bat when you lighten up. As you cover the water on your favorite lake, pond or stream, the fish are actually going to tell you when there's a bass nearby that's ready to bite.

Especially when fishing with jigs, soft plastics and little crankbaits, you're probably going to catch—or, at least, get bites from—a dozen members of the other species for every bass you encounter. But along the way, you'll start to understand how these smaller fish can help you figure out what's going on and where the bass are.

I've been using ultralight gear and baits on bass waters for more than thirty years. But it wasn't until spending more than half that time on the water that I started to see how the other fish that shared a given lake or pond with the bass were tipping me off.

For example, crappies and sunfish are smaller than bass, but they're still predators. They're going to use the same kinds of cover and take up the same kinds of ambush positions as bass would—if they were around.

When you work through a given section of shoreline cover and only catch bluegills or orange-spotted sunfish or other panfish, don't get discouraged. Instead, acknowledge that one of two things may be the cause of your problem:

Small fish caught while fishing for bass give the angler a clue to which predators are using that specific location.

1. You are fishing the bait you've chosen the way you should to get bass to bite because the predators that are in this neighborhood are showing interest. It's just the bass that aren't biting.

2. All the bass are somewhere else.

You'll find out where that is when you start moving through another, similar area and the little fish don't bite.

Think about it: We all know that sunfish, crappies, bluegills, perch and any other small fish in a given lake will act like bass when they can get away with it. But they're going to be wary at best, or gone altogether, when bass start using the area—the small fish sense naturally that their status has changed from predator to prey. It's at these times that you should be alert to the possibility of a big ol' bass preparing to strike whatever it is you're fishing.

Does it always happen this way? No, but my experience suggests that it doesn't only because the bass in a spot are more negative in mood.

I've never had a bluegill take an ultralight bass bait away from a largemouth. Never. I've never caught a sunfish on one cast and a bass on the next from the same spot—or vice versa.

But over the years, I've fished plenty of spots multiple times where, on one visit, I caught several little fish, but on the next, I caught a bass without a little fish nearby. The next time, I got no bites at all. That's when I believe the bass are still there, but not interested in hitting.

As you learn about the ultralight baits that catch bass and how you should fish them, keep these on-the-water keys in mind. As you become more sensitive to what's going on when you're actually on the water, you're going to become a better angler.

and a motto that seems almost too simple to be true—"You can't fish 'em wrong," it goes, "as long as you fish 'em slow." It's true—not only for Road Runners, but for any UL bass jig you can think of.

The Natural Look

It all has to do with the general approach that is most effective when fishing jigs and soft plastics on ultralight gear for bass. That approach is rooted in the word natural.

No matter how large or small your favorite bass pond, lake or stream is, so many of the baitfish that bass dine on have absolutely nothing wrong with them! They're not injured; they're perfectly fine. Their only mistake usually involves being in the wrong place at the wrong time and getting too close to a largemouth or smallmouth waiting in ambush.

Can you imagine how long a lunker would go between meals if it only ate the injured or otherwise weak? Give your favorite gamefish credit for being a lot smarter and more resourceful than that.

And when you're fishing jigs on ultralight gear, give your baits a more natural look than you're probably used to. The term jig, when used as a verb, means to move your bait up and down fairly erratically, doesn't it? But you don't need to do that to catch fish. And if you change your approach to one that provides a more natural look, you might even start catching more bass more often!

Road Runners are jigs that imitate baitfish. You also can use jig heads with soft-plastic bodies to achieve the same look. I fish the Blakemore

Jigs

When most anglers hear the words bass and jig in the same sentence these days, their minds generally envision fish holding tight to thick, heavy cover. And they imagine heavy pitching and flipping gear with 1/2-ounce (14-g) or heavier jigs tipped with pork chunks or plastic trailers—the vererable jig and pig—tied onto 17- or 20-pound (7.6- to 9-kg) line.

Bass fans who choose UL tackle have a lot more jigging

options than they might realize. Jigging for bass doesn't just mean pitching or flipping to heavy cover with heavy gear. Although very effective during a cold front or when water temperatures are fairly low, those aren't the only ways jigs catch bass. And they're not the only jigs bass hit hard and often.

Oklahoma bass fishing legend and TV host Jimmy Houston has, for years, been touting the merits of Road Runners. Made by Blakemore Lure Company, these little jigs feature a spinner blade just below the jig head bait—or one like it—whenever I choose to fish this style of jig because of that spinner blade. With it there, you don't have to impart any action at all to get some extra flash.

My favorite place to fish jigs like this one is along shorelines that have a lot of weedy cover, as opposed to rocks. That flooded vegetation attracts baitfish like a magnet because of the available plankton, which are minnows' bread and butter.

And this is fishing about as easy as it gets. Cast the lure near the edges of the weeds or shore, then simply swim it slowly back to you. If you're fishing from shore and casting out into deeper water, try to keep a tight line on the bait as it falls slowly to the bottom. Often, fish will hit it as it falls, just as they would if you were fishing from a boat and casting it along a steep drop-off.

I bet the toughest part of this kind of jig fishing for you will be not adding extra action on your retrieves. Your brain is telling you there's a jig on the end of that line and you ought to be jigging it. Don't! Instead, imagine the look of a baitfish moving along without a care in the world, seconds before a nice bass ambushes it. That's the look and feel you want; and the only way to get it is with a slow, steady, natural retrieve.

If you're reading this chapter because you prefer bass to any other species, then it's likely the jigs you're most familiar with are what I call the traditional flipping-and-pitching jigs like those made by Stanley and Strike King, among others.

They have fairly heavy heads and wide-gap hooks, with living rubber or other synthetic skirts.

Weedlines are one of the best places to fish a jig with a spinner blade.

You tip them with pork or soft plastic trailers, make short casts into heavy cover and move them up and down.

Have you ever thought about fishing them as if they were live crawfish? On ultralight tackle, they are very effective. I never fish steep, rocky structure without slowly walking a jig and trailer combo naturally through the rocks; just like crawfish do.

If that doesn't work, I won't give up until I try the other surefire bass jig for ultralight fishing—a "creature-style" soft plastic body on a 1/8- or 1/4-ounce (3.5- or 7-g) stand-up jig head.

My all-time favorite plastic for this technique is the twin-tail creature-style grub made by Gary Yamamoto. They're expensive and soft enough that you'll tear one up catching no more than two or three keepers. But

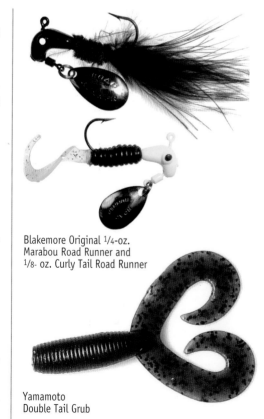

Blakemore Original 1/4-oz. Marabou Road Runner and 1/8- oz. Curly Tail Road Runner

Yamamoto Double Tail Grub

they work—especially the color Yamamoto calls "bluegill." I've seen with my own eyes that, especially in fairly clear water, this color mimics a real crawfish with amazing accuracy. Largemouths, smallmouths and spotted bass all just seem to love it.

I could probably make the case that these three baits—a swimming baitfish imitator like Blakemore's Road Runner, a traditional flipping jig and trailer, and a grub on a stand-up head—are the only lures you need to catch bass on every outing with ultralight gear. But I also can—and will—make the case that some anglers just plain enjoy fishing other bass baits. And they all work in ultralight sizes and weights.

Soft Plastics

You can catch bass on UL tackle and lures using every kind of soft-plastic presentation there is—Texas rigs, Carolina rigs, soft-plastic jerkbaits, tube baits, you name it!

And chances are, if you're a serious bass angler, you already know it. You've just always heard it referred to as "finesse" fishing. I prefer to think of it as anytime, anywhere bass fishing because I prefer the ultralight approach.

A generation ago, Tennessean Charlie Brewer introduced the world to this kind of bassin' with his Slider worm rig. Using a fairly standard worm hook with a smooth, relatively flat lead head at its front, Brewer Texas-rigged 4-inch (10-cm) worms and fished them very naturally on ultralight gear. He wrote a book all about it (*Charlie Brewer On Slider Fishin'*) and that volume validated a lot of what I learned over the years through trial and error.

If anything, when fishing worms, tube baits and jerkbaits, the only element of finesse I employ comes to my retrieve. I don't consider lightening up an element of finesse. But just like using jigs in open water to imitate crawfish, I like to fish these kinds of baits as if they're not injured and just going about their routine, but ending up in the wrong place at the wrong time. You'll know you've succeeded with every bite!

"Say Cheese!"

My phone rang late one Friday night, and the magazine editor on the other end of the line was in a pickle. He had a story I filed months earlier with his predecessor, and he wanted to use it in the next issue of his monthly, which was going to press in about ten days.

"I have the cutlines for the photos you sent," he said, "but I can't find the photos anywhere. Can you get some new ones in the mail by Monday or Tuesday?"

"Sure thing," I answered. "They'll be on their way to you no later than Tuesday." All I had to do was go catch some nice bass and reshoot them! Another quick phone call set up a trip with a coworker the next morning, to Osage State Fishing Lake in central Kansas. I knew there were plenty of bass there, but I also knew that they got quite a bit of fishing pressure.

On the 45-minute drive early the next morning, we talked about where and how we'd start fishing. Osage SFL has one true main-lake point; it's fairly steep and rocky. On a lark, I tied a 1/4-ounce (7-g) "flipping jig" on and added a piece of pork. As the bow of the boat eased within range of the point, I made a cast toward its very tip, paying more attention to boat position than the bait as it settled toward the bottom.

When I was satisfied that we were in the right spot to really start fishing, I reeled in the slack line to find a 3-pound (1.4-kg) largemouth already hooked and ready to fight! First cast; on a jig cast to open shoreline featuring the kind of structure that crawfish love.

We caught a few more and took some photos. I knew the editor would be happy with the results—I sure was.

Blakemore 6" pre-rigged purple worm (top) and 4" panfish worm (bottom)

Pre-Rigged Worms

When it comes to ultralight bassin' using soft plastics, I have a secret weapon. It's one that's been around since I was a kid, and one that many "serious" anglers probably walk by when tackle shopping without so much as a second thought.

It's those pre-rigged 6-inch (15-cm) worms with hooks, head and tail, and with a tiny two-bladed prop and some orange plastic beads at the head. Creme made the first one I ever used, back in the 1960s. And those folks at Blakemore made the one that fooled the largest bass I've ever hooked.

Although I'm sure it will work as well as a Texas-rigged worm, I generally make it an alternate to the venerable Carolina rig instead. I fish it along the edges of weedlines and on flats that hold bass. And whenever possible, I use a presentation similar to those I use with spinnerbaits or topwater plugs. I cast it beyond the structure I want to fish, then bring it through the area in the strike zone, keeping it there as long as I can.

During one late-summer outing on a lake that was several feet low due to lack of rain, I happened on an old tree trunk lying along one edge of the channel. Getting the boat into position, I threw the worm about 10 feet (3 m) past the far end of the tree, then slowly swam it back along the structure.

All at once, my line just started moving off. I never felt a strike, even on the light tackle. The bass just inhaled the bait and started swimming off with it. I let it swim all the slack out of the line, then just tightened up on it. When it felt resistance, it went nuts! And the lack of a strong hookset cost me dearly.

After only a moment, more than 2 feet (60 cm) of largemouth broke through the surface film, and it shook its head in defiance, spitting the worm back at me before taking off!

Texas and Carolina Rigging

Now, when it comes to Texas and Carolina rigs, going ultralight means primarily using lighter weights. I don't fish these rigs any differently than I would with a heavy casting outfit spooled with 17-pound-test (7.6-kg) and casting 3/8- or 1/2-ounce (10.6- or 14-g) lures.

I have started rigging them a little differently, though. It's a trick that I'll use on any Texas or Carolina rig I fish from now on, regardless of its size or weight. When adding the worm, I rig it like most anglers rig a soft-plastic jerkbait; that is, I expose the

Ultralight fishing for bass with this Carolina-rigged lizard is the same as so-called "finesse fishing" methods. Weights are usually lighter, however.

point of the hook on the top side of the worm. As a result, hooksets have become virtually effortless, and I lose far fewer fish.

Jerkbaits

We must not forget the relatively new soft-plastic jerkbait. Even a 6-inch (15-cm) Slug-Go, when fished only on a hook, will meet the ultralight muster. They are great fun to fish, especially from the end of the spawn through the beginning of summer's dog days. It's during this time that bass anglers generally enjoy the best of the season's topwater action, and these baits are killer as a result.

Color

When it comes to picking colors, I've come to believe over the years that much of it is angler preference. I fish purple worms more often than any other color, regardless of the rigging I'm using or the relative water clarity because it's the color I have the most confidence in.

Alabaman Tom Mann, who just might be the father of today's plastic worms—remember Mann's Jelly Worms?—laughs when he tells folks who ask that he fishes every color there is, as long as it's black! I feel the same way about purple when it comes to worms.

If I decide to Carolina-rig a lizard instead of a worm, I go

with a pumpkinseed body sporting a chartreuse tail. I've seen way too many fish caught on this color lizard to opt for anything else.

In tube baits, I stick with purple, pumpkinseed or chartreuse. The latter is my first choice in really off-color water. Over time, I've developed confidence in these combinations. I believe fish will hit them, and they usually do. When you start thinking about colors, I doubt you'll go wrong by sticking with those shades you have the most confidence in.

For jerkbaits, rainbow trout, when I can find it, is my first choice in color. For some reason, bass just love it!

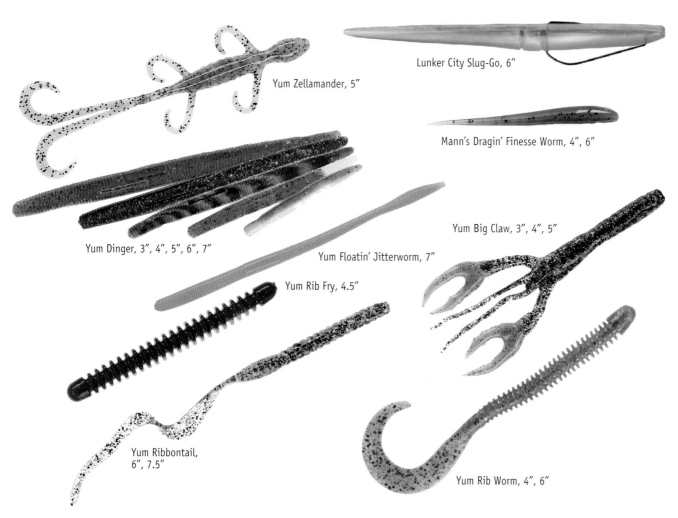

Yum Zellamander, 5"

Lunker City Slug-Go, 6"

Mann's Dragin' Finesse Worm, 4", 6"

Yum Dinger, 3", 4", 5", 6", 7"

Yum Big Claw, 3", 4", 5"

Yum Floatin' Jitterworm, 7"

Yum Rib Fry, 4.5"

Yum Ribbontail, 6", 7.5"

Yum Rib Worm, 4", 6"

Spinners

My first choice in a safety-spin-style spinnerbait for bass is a 1/4-ounce (7-g) model with two willowleaf blades. White, chartreuse and the white/chartreuse combination are the only colors I use—and the latter two are saved only for the darkest days and/or the most off-color water.

I find the best action with these baits in three different situations: close to shore, through treetops and near bluffs.

Booyah Blade Double Willow, 1/4 oz.

Close to Shore

This strategy involves gently sloping backs that feature gravel bottoms or weeds. I position the boat so that my longest cast gets within a few inches (centimeters) of the shore, and I fish the bait back to the boat as quickly as I need to so that it's no more than 2 to 3 inches (5- to 7.6-cm) below the surface. If fish don't react, I slow the lure down and bump it along the bottom.

Through Treetops

Fishing through the tops of flooded trees also is a great way to go ultralight spinnerbaiting. This is an approach that works best when you can position yourself to cast several feet (meters) beyond your target and keep the bait working in the strike zone as long as possible.

When fishing through treetops, it pays to pause your retrieve when you bump a branch, or anytime you get close to one. Bass often smack the bait hard during this pause. And for some reason, my experience has been that a pause just after the spinnerbait clears the tree and heads out into open water will trigger strikes.

Near Bluffs

Of all the spinnerbaiting I've done, however, nothing beats paralleling a bluff bank in the late summer and fall. A former tournament partner, Steve Holland, taught me the fine points of this approach during a few seasons of team tournaments on Table Rock Lake and Bull Shoals Lake, in southwest Missouri and northwest Arkansas. Holland grew up in Forsyth, Missouri, and knows both lakes as few others do.

And I've never seen anyone fish a spinnerbait on a bluff bank as effectively as he can. Lots of anglers do it, but few use Holland's philosophy. He just doesn't believe you can fish the lure too close to the bluff, and I've seen him catch way too many keepers to argue.

Holland made no bones about the fact that, when we were fishing tournaments together, I wasn't going to get much of a chance on the bluffs because of the way he positioned the boat. I made up for it at other spots during the day; but along the bluffs, I generally watched him more than I fished!

Holland's goal was to make as long a cast as possible, with his spinnerbait literally scraping the bluff as it tumbled into the water. He immediately began his retrieve, often bulging—but not breaking—the surface film with the whirling willow leaf blades. When his bait got more than 3 to 4 inches (7.6 to 10 cm) from the bluff, he pretty much reeled in as fast as he could and made another cast.

Largemouths, smallmouths and spotted bass all came drifting up from their suspended hideouts to take his offerings, and we cashed more than a few checks as a result of his bluff-fishing prowess.

What I like best about this technique is its perfect adaptability to ultralight gear. There are no obstructions or snags to worry about because you're fishing what amounts to open water, for fish that are suspended along the bluffs. It's simply a killer approach to ultralight bass fishing on any lake that has bluff banks.

Dunlap No. 2

An ultralight, safety-pin-style spinnerbait provided me with the best evening of bass fishing I enjoyed as a teenager, and one of the best ever. I remember the scene as if it happened yesterday....

Some Pennsylvania governmental agency had decided to build a second flood-control lake on Dunlap Creek in Fayette County, just a couple of ridges and valleys northwest of the little coal-mining "patch" I grew up in. Dunlap No. 1 had been a favorite fishing spot for a few years, and was where I learned how crappies depend so much on structure and how good purple was when it came to fishing plastic worms for bass.

When Dunlap No. 2 started filling, bass and panfish were stocked, and the fishing action took off from the get-go. Word got out that bass were absolutely slamming Beetle Spins, an ultralight spinnerbait that, at that time, was still pretty new. The yellow and black ones worked great; then, somebody discovered a locally produced version with a gold body that was even better.

Back then, the local hotspot for bait and tackle was, of all things, an auto parts store. To this day, Frank's Auto, in Uniontown, Pennsylvania, still devotes the same corner of its retail space to fishing tackle and baits. Frank's had the spinners for Dunlap No. 2, so I got a couple and headed out there one late-spring evening.

State fish biologists had planted several large brush piles before the lake started filling, and one of them was along the steep bank of a little notch on the lake's north side. There must have been bass crawling all over that structure because I never made a cast into the setting sun that evening without at least getting a bite. The action was nonstop; I only left when there wasn't enough natural light to see.

And despite several return trips, I never saw that kind of action again. Maybe the fish got educated or maybe other folks were keeping fish instead of releasing them all as I had.

I have, however, continued to enjoy regular success with ultralight spinnerbaits ever since. And it's been a joy in recent years to see so many manufacturers either keep or add 1/4-ounce (7-g) models of what has become the stereotypical bass spinnerbait. It's been more than ten years since I made a cast with one heavier. In reality, there's no need to.

Crankbaits

What you've read so far, I hope, makes a good case for using an ultralight approach on just about any kind of bass fishing you enjoy. But I've saved the best for last because no other form of bass fishing lends itself to the ultralight approach better than crankbaiting.

The reason is simple: Ultralight crankbaits are everywhere these days! Every type—divers, topwaters and stickbaits—is available in sizes weighing 1/4 ounce (7 g) or less. And all of them work just as effectively on bass— even the biggest of bass—as

their larger counterparts.

My all-time favorite crankbait is the ultralight craw-fish imitation made and sold under the Rebel brand by Arkansas-based PRADCO. Its 77 series, which I know and love as the "Wee-Craw," is sold in shallow-diving (2 to 3 feet/0.6 to 0.9 m) and deep-diving (4 to 6 feet/1.2 to 1.8 m) models in a variety of colors.

I absolutely swear by two colors with this lure—No. 60, which is a green "stream" craw-dad imitation, and No. 34, which is chartreuse with a bright orange belly. I use the former in all but the most off-color water, which is where I throw the latter.

When it comes to bass, I also throw Bill Lewis' smallest Rat-L-Trap, the 1/8-ounce (3.5-g) Tiny Trap, quite often. It's a great choice on lakes with some weedy shoreline cover, and also during those times of year when there are significant schools of small baitfish available.

Maybe the most difficult element of this discussion is including all of the ultralight crankbaits that will catch bass. So many are available these days, it's amazing. In addition to PRADCO (which makes Rebel and several other brands) and Bill Lewis, you can find them made by Rapala, Yo-Zuri, Bass Pro

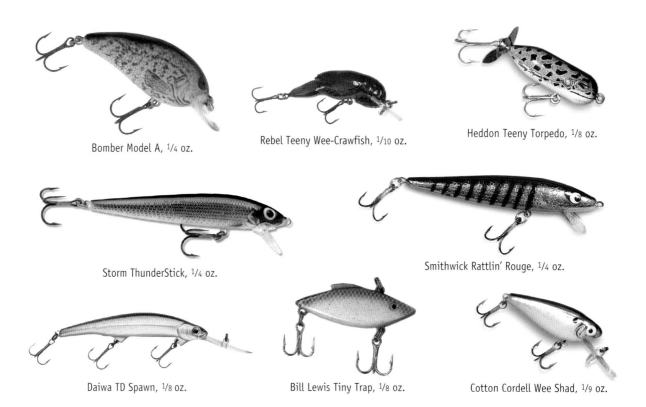

Bomber Model A, 1/4 oz.

Rebel Teeny Wee-Crawfish, 1/10 oz.

Heddon Teeny Torpedo, 1/8 oz.

Storm ThunderStick, 1/4 oz.

Smithwick Rattlin' Rouge, 1/4 oz.

Daiwa TD Spawn, 1/8 oz.

Bill Lewis Tiny Trap, 1/8 oz.

Cotton Cordell Wee Shad, 1/9 oz.

Shops, Reef Runner, Daiwa, Cabela's, Worden's, Gaines Phillips, Storm, Berkley, and many more manufacturers.

You'll find examples of all three crankbait types (divers, topwaters and stickbaits) in sizes weighing 1/4 ounce (7 g) or less. That means you can go ultralight no matter how you prefer to fish crankbaits.

Have I tried all of them? No. Do I have any reason to believe any of them won't catch bass? No.

Plain and simple, bass of all sizes are predators and, as such, opportunistic feeders. If you put a bait in the strike zone and a bass in a positive or neutral feeding mood is nearby, there's a good chance you'll get a strike. If the fish are negative, it frankly won't matter much what you throw or how big it is. Negative fish generally aren't going to bite.

If you want a "guide" to

fishing ultralight crankbaits for bass, I ask that you develop your own because you likely already know everything you need to. If you've fished crankbaits for bass, you can already handle the ultralight approach. All you have to do, most likely, is get some smaller baits and switch to a UL bass outfit.

If you enjoy fishing diving-baitfish imitations, get the smaller versions in the colors you prefer. If stickbaits do it for you, go with the ultralight stickbaits. And yes, you can weight them to suspend just as you do with full-size lures for prespawn action.

Admittedly, doing so will probably take you beyond the 1/4-ounce (7-g) limit for baits I've been discussing. Choosing to proceed is up to you. If it were me, I'd likely go with a diving crankbait and fish it erratically, or even opt for a

spinnerbait because prespawn bass will tear it up.

Fall, however, is when ultralight stickbaits fished on the surface with a twitchy, erratic retrieve are very effective. They also work when fished like this during the postspawn period. Don't dismiss them. Just fish them when their natural tendencies put the odds in your favor.

Although I've already said for the record that the Wee-Craw is my top producer, I also have to admit that no ultralight crankbaits excite me more than topwater plugs. Poppers are my first choices because I have more confidence in my ability to fish them effectively than with "walking" baits like the Zara Spook. But the latter style is available in ultralight sizes, and they work just as well as their larger, heavier brethren for those who can fish them well.

Bass Heaven

When it comes to numbers, a Rebel ultralight Pop-R contributed to the finest day of bass fishing I've ever enjoyed.

Rebel Pop-R, 1/8 oz.

It happened one warm May day several years ago during the annual spring meeting of the Outdoor Writers of Kansas.

We convened in the southeast corner of the state, which is home to hundreds of old strip-mine pits that have been reclaimed for fishing and outdoor recreation—some by private landowners, others by the state's Department of Wildlife and Parks.

I used the same rod-and-reel combo I had in the float tube, the spincast reel spooled with 6-pound (2.7-kg) line, and started the day by Carolina-rigging. In this case, that meant crimping-on a split shot about 20 inches (50 cm) above my hook, which sported a 4-inch (10-cm) worm. I had a box full of the little plastic baits in a virtual rainbow of colors.

I caught a foot-long (30-cm) largemouth on my first cast, and that set the tone for the day. From mid-morning until late afternoon, I caught literally dozens of bass between 1 and 2 1/2 pounds (0.45 and 1 kg)—and used every color I had along with success. My guide, whose family owned the land with the pits we fished, got to laughing at me when I decided to see whether I could catch at least one bass on every color. I joined him in the laughter when I did.

We'd changed pits late in the day and were just pushing away from shore when I caught movement out of the corner of my eye and looked left just in time to see a fish swirl at the surface near a flooded log along the far shore. On a hunch, I put away the worms and weights, replacing them with an ultralight Pop-R in fire tiger. From then until we couldn't see to fish any more that evening, I caught bass after bass on the surface. Everywhere I thought there ought to be a bass, there was.

And at the end of the most prolific fishing day I've ever enjoyed, I was thrilled—but not a bit tired. Ultralight fishing never wears you out; it just fires you up a little more with every fish you hook.

Chapter 5

Crappies and Other Panfish

When it comes to ultralight tackle, many anglers will tell you they love to use it when they go fishing for a big mess of crappies or bluegills. And what do they usually use? Hooks, bobbers and live bait.

What a shame. There can be so much more to taking these fish with ultralight gear—tricks and techniques that will add loads of fun to every trip you make.

Here's the key: You have to start thinking of these scrappy little fighters as the predators they truly are. If you do, your world will open up to all kinds of options when it comes to catching them.

Jigs

Unless you're hopelessly addicted to fishing live bait under a bobber, it's likely that you have caught panfish on jigs. But there's a good chance you haven't been very creative about it.

You've probably used tiny UL gear and the smallest jigs you could find because you know that's what catches little sunfish and crappies. That's true, but just as true is the fact that many species of sunfish and black and white crappies, grow to really good sizes.

There is a pecking order, just as with any species of fish or game. And those that grow big, strong and healthy are going to react quickly to larger jigs. One big meal can replace a lot of little ones.

You simply have to start approaching these smallest of freshwater gamefish as predators, just as you do the trout,

bass, pike or walleye you also enjoy catching. Admittedly, they're smaller than these other species; but that doesn't make them any less susceptible to being fooled.

You have a tremendous variety of options when it comes to fishing jigs for crappies and other panfish. Don't just limit yourself to those tiny micro jigs that are miniature versions of the tube baits that have become so popular for bass.

Yes, of course, those micro jigs work. But so do larger baits. And the bigger the bait, the better your chance of fooling a real slabside.

One of the best all-around panfish lures you'll ever use is a 3-inch (7.62-cm) grub with either a curly tail or a paddle tail. The former offers an enticing action, especially when fished super slowly. The latter, especially in lighter shades, mimics baitfish that crappies, rock bass and big bluegills feed on.

Large sunfish are no different than any other predatory gamefish. They will take the best possible ambush spots in a given area. And once you locate those spots, you can take big slabsides from there time after time.

Recent fishing seasons also have seen the introduction of smaller plastic crawdad bodies. When fished along rocky cover using 1/16- or 1/8-ounce (1.7- or 3.5-g) heads, these baits stimulate consistent, almost nonstop attention from panfish.

School Fishing

Think back to when you were a kid, fishing for sunfish with a can of small worms and a bobber above your hook. It's the way many of us first enjoyed time on the water or at its edge.

Remember how you'd find a spot where there seemed to be so many fish that you couldn't catch all of them? And remember how you'd often fish that same spot over and over again, and always seem to find action there? I call that "school fishing."

Chances are that, today, you understand why that occurred—and you even use that knowledge when you have a chance to introduce new or young anglers to the joys of fishing. You know that all the panfish species tend to school up, and they also tend to use the same structures throughout a given body of water.

If you're fishing a lake or stream, or a specific area on one, for the first time, you can take a trick from the bass anglers' bible and use it to make the most of every panfish outing. That is, use a faster-moving bait to locate panfish; then, slow down and fish them thoroughly with jigs. It's an approach that always pays off.

Although they're among the smallest of all the panfish, orange-spotted sunfish are special to me because they are so striking in appearance, and they are amazing little fighters. For sheer enjoyment, I'd rather catch them than just about any other fish that swims because, ounce for ounce, they are plain tough customers.

All sunfish tend to school, and all of them tend to relate to similar, if not the same, structures around a given body of water. Once you learn those spots, you can enjoy regular action.

Orange-Spots

For nine fishing seasons, I called a public lake in the Kansas City area home when it came to fishing. Orange-spotted sunfish lived there, and they always used certain areas. There was one fairly small section of weed-choked shoreline that I could always count on when I wanted to catch of few of them. To this day, I can't explain why that particular species of sunfish was drawn to that particular part of the lake more than any other.

The same weeds grew in the same way in other areas, but it was rare to catch an orange-spot anywhere else on this 250-acre (100-hectare) impoundment. It also was home to bluegills, green sunfish, and black and white crappies. All of them used similar structure around the lake; but they never seemed to hang out where the orange-spots were.

I found these colorful little slabsides on one of the first trips I ever made to this lake, more than twenty years ago. And after a season of always picking them up in the same 50-or-so-yard (45.5-m) stretch of shoreline, I began doing just what I've suggested here with jigs.

Whenever I wanted to catch some orange-spots, I showed up at the lake with a 3-inch (7.6-cm) grub, usually in purple, on a 1/16- or 1/8-ounce (1.7- or 3.5-g) jig head. I went lighter early in the season, before the water warmed up, because all the fish in the lake tended to be sluggish and reacted best to a slow presentation. From mid-May through mid-October, however, there was no need to slow down. Often, my jig seemed to fall right into one of these fish's mouths because one would smack the lure literally as it was hitting the water.

This fishing was exciting and predictable, which is something many anglers wish for. The fish made it exciting by their very nature. Through their reaction to jigs (once I realized they had a "honey hole" on this lake), they showed me how predictable they could be.

This story is important because the concepts don't just apply to orange-spots.

And to learn those spots, all you have to do is pay attention to where you pick up bluegills or crappies on the places you fish. Make note of them, and spend some time studying the area. If a topographic map is available, all the better because it'll help you see exactly what kind of structure or shoreline breaks these little fighters are relating to.

Once you've done this kind of homework, it's time to fish some jigs. If you haven't done much of this, you should expect certain and different kinds of reactions during periods of coldwater versus warmwater temperatures. Early and late in the season, panfish hit very lightly, and you generally get strikes as you crawl your bait along the bottom or swim it through the brush pile, if that's what you're fishing.

Later on, during that mid-May to mid-October period, you should (1) expect a strike on every cast because the action can get that fast-paced and (2) expect strikes to be aggressive and immediate. Fish are warm-blooded and, as such, become more aggressive from late spring through early fall. When the water warms up, so do they; their metabolism quickens, and they need more food to get through a day. Maybe because they somehow realize that their diminutive size (when compared to, say, bass or walleyes or pike) makes them the collective "low man" on the feeding totem pole in a given body of water, they are quick to snatch any easy meal that comes by.

Big Jig, Small Hook

You might be surprised at how big a lure these little fish will hit. When it comes to catching them, it's not so much that you keep the bait small. Rather, you should make sure you have hooks small enough to hit home when the fish bite and you react.

If you don't believe it, rig a 3- or 4-inch (7.6- or 10-cm) curly-tail grub, in your choice of color, on a small jig head and fish it where you know there are panfish. They're going to hit it, and you're going to catch them on lures that sometimes aren't

Riverside Lures Grub with Gopher Tackle Connie Jig, 1/16 oz.

Lindy Fuzz-E Grub (1/32 oz. to 1/8 oz.) and The Queen (1/32 oz. and 1/16 oz.)

much smaller than they are. It's the fierce nature of these little fighters that has kept me coming back for more, season after season.

There's also another reason to make larger jigs a part of your ultralight arsenal: Every lake you fish probably has crappies and panfish a lot bigger than you'll ever know—unless you try to catch them on these bigger baits.

The next time you start getting into nice schools of fish, try this: Move away to the best-looking adjacent cover you can find, and start fishing a large jig as you would if you were after keeper bass or walleyes. You might be sur-

prised with the strike of a really nice crappie or panfish.

What I'm suggesting here is a spot that features the same general kind of cover as the area holding good numbers of smaller fish, but one that might only be big enough to hold a few average-size specimens—or one really big one. More often than not, the latter will be there, and you'll have a chance to catch it by thinking of it as a bona fide predatory gamefish.

Once you've become accustomed to the spots on your favorite lake or pond that hold these bigger fish, you'll be able to go there again and again and get strikes. Nature dictates that if you remove a dominant fish

from a given area, another dominant fish will replace it.

If you bass fish, you know there are certain spots that always hold keepers. If you trout fish, you know that certain pools and deep runs in a stream or river always hold the biggest rainbows and browns.

It's the same with crappies, bluegills and other sunfish. The biggest fish are going to keep using the best ambush spots, and they aren't always going to be a part of areas where schools of smaller fish concentrate. Taking the time to fish a larger jig around likely-looking spots is going to make you better because it's going to teach you where the big ones like to hang out.

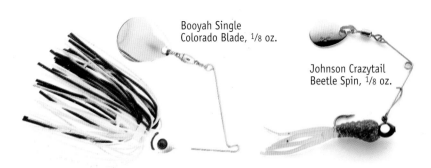
Booyah Single
Colorado Blade, 1/8 oz.

Johnson Crazytail
Beetle Spin, 1/8 oz.

Panther Martin inline spinner, 1/8 oz.

Spinners

The smallest of safety-pin-style spinners, like the well-known Beetle Spin made by Johnson, really come into their own when it comes to panfish and crappies. They are effective and among the easiest of baits to fish properly. That makes them great candidates for use whenever you take someone on their first fishing trip.

And to me, there is no better place to fish spinners for panfish and crappies than on warmwater streams. Maybe it's just me but the fish seem so much more aggressive when it comes to hitting a spinnerbait in moving water than their lake-bound brethren.

That's not to say that spinners won't work in lakes; they do, all season long. But on streams and rivers where crappies and other panfish live, spinners give you a chance to effectively fish any kind of water you encounter.

Streams

You're on a stream, for example, and you look above or below you to see an obviously deep pool at a dogleg in the channel. That is, a riffle or deeper run is dumping water into a hole just where the stream bends, making a definite current with easy-to-see breaks and an eddy on one side of the pool.

Regardless of the size of the stream, here's what you can expect at that hole: There will be some kind of brush or other fish-holding structure just below the head of the pool, in its deepest part. Because there's a bend in the channel here, periods of high water are washing limbs, brush and other "junk" into the hole, and some of it ends up staying deep when the water recedes. The downstream side of that structure will have a current break, and fish will be waiting there in ambush.

They'll also be holding wherever they can along the current

break throughout the entire length of the pool, lying just off the edge of the fastest moving water waiting to nail any easy meal that comes drifting or swimming by. And finally, they'll be in the eddy created away from the current. So there are three possible places in a given hole for panfish to be; and it's hard to beat a spinner for finding out which of them the fish are using.

By their very natures, inline and safety-pin-style lures can be fished at virtually any depth simply by varying the start and rate of your retrieve. You can let the bait sink to the deepest part of the hole and keep it there with a slow crank of your reel handle. Or, you can cast it literally right against the far bank and, using a fast retrieve, bring the spinner across the hole either rippling or just under the surface.

Lakes and Ponds

It's hard to match the spinner's versatility when you're after panfish in streams. And it's just as tough to overestimate their value on lakes and ponds, although some anglers never seem to think of them when they're after crappies and other panfish.

If, for example, you're fishing a farm pond in mid- to late summer, you're likely going to find at least a stand or two of grass or weeds somewhere. Or maybe you know of a lake with coves or even larger bays full of lily pads or other aquatic vegetation.

Bass fishermen head straight for spots like that. So do anglers after pike. And if you enjoy catching panfish and have some ultralight spinners, you shouldn't let those other folks have all the fun!

Spinners are great to use in spots like these. Beetle Spin–

style baits are especially good because they are more weed resistant than inline models, which usually are equipped with treble hooks. The latter are OK in lily pads, but can get hung up a lot in thicker vegetation. Spinners also take all kinds of panfish and crappies in more open water when you fish them around and over brush piles or other man-made fish attractors.

When it comes to size, you'll find a mix of 1/8- and 1/4-ounce (3.5- and 7-g) spinners in the box I use for crappies and panfish. The lighter-weight ones are my first choice. But on streams and rivers during periods of high, swift water, the extra weight of the 1/4-ounce versions can make the difference. Crappies and other panfish must believe these lures are baitfish because white and yellow lures with silver blades have proven to be my bread-and-butter baits.

Locate schools of panfish near some weedy cover with a safety-pin-style spinnerbait.

CRAPPIES AND OTHER PANFISH

Switch out any jig
that you like with a Beetle-spin-style spinner. It gives you a little versatility to make any type of smaller spinnerbait you like.

Two Secrets

There are a couple of "secrets" you need to know to make the most out of your crappie and panfish trips when using spinners. The first is that you can turn any jig you own into a spinner if you use Beetle Spin–style rigs with snaps on the business end. Many anglers haven't tried them, but they definitely work. You open the snap, slide the line eye of your jig head on, close the snap, and you have a safety-pin-style spinner of your own design.

The other secret is that there's a bait—and it's been around for generations—that also combines the best of jig and spinner fishing: the Road Runner. The specific bait of that name is made and sold by Blakemore Lures. There are other manufacturers making similar lures on the market, but none of them come in the variety of colors and bodies that Road Runners do. You'll find them with maribou bodies, curly-tail grubs, tube-style bodies. All of them feature a spinner blade on the jig head, just below the line tie.

For years, Blakemore's marketing slogan has been the same when it comes to Road Runners: "You can't fish 'em wrong as long as you fish 'em slow." As much a part of this secret is my own personal twist on that idea: You can fish 'em faster and also be fishing 'em right.

I include them in this section on spinners, instead of in the earlier section on jigs because Road Runners can be fished with a steady, swimming retrieve just like any other spinner with surprisingly good results on crappies and other panfish. I've taken rock bass in streams using this method, and crappies and other species in lakes when swimming the lure around and through submerged brush piles.

Road Runner
Marabou, 1/32 oz.

Road Runner
Curly Tail, 1/32 oz.

Road Runner
Mr. Crappie, 1/8 oz.

Crankbaits

If you were to gather a hundred anglers into a room and ask them to list their favorite baits for crappies and panfish, I'd be willing to bet you that none of them would include crankbaits. But I contend that ultralight crankbaits can be as effective at taking crappies and other species of panfish as any other bait.

The largest black and white crappies I've ever caught hit ultralight crankbaits. The black one came from a steep, rocky shoreline and was taken on a crawdad imitation. The white one bolted from some shoreline weeds to inhale a tiny minnow imitation.

Neither was the first crappie I'd ever taken like this, and they sure weren't the last. Make no mistake—panfish are predators; and as such, they'll hit ultralight crankbaits without hesitation. They're not too picky about it, either. That is, they don't seem to prefer one particular style of lure over another. They hit 'em all, and often.

One of the things you'll learn about these tasty little gamefish when you start chasing them with ultralight crankbaits is that there are exceptions to the rules of how they act. That is, some of the largest members of every species aren't going to be schooled up with the bunches of their smaller relatives.

Experience has shown me that they like to strike out on their own, and they begin acting very much like bass, pike and other, much larger predators. They take up ambush points and use holding positions that, while related to some kind of structure, aren't conducive to schooling fish.

I've taken big crappies and huge sunfish along logs in 6 to 8 feet (1.8 to 2.4 m) of water; the kinds of places where you'd expect to find bass. I've taken them off rocks, like the black crappie mentioned earlier, and from tiny patches of weeds, like the white crappie also mentioned earlier.

Treat Them Like Bass

Maybe the easiest way to describe my mindset when fishing ultralight crankbaits for big crappies and panfish is this—I "bass fish" for them. Along the way, I often do catch some bass, too. But this approach pays big dividends in the form of big crappies and panfish.

When I approach a given stretch of shoreline, I like to focus on making presentations parallel to trees that have fallen into the water. I run the lure across the front of weedlines, or over the tops of them if they're just under the surface.

I pay particular attention to even the smallest of breaks or changes in the shoreline—like a little cut, or a spot where runoff flows into the lake and, as a result, keeps the weeds from growing there. Any kind of edge or change in an otherwise routine stretch of bank is likely to hold a big crappie or panfish, and crankbaits are perfect lures to use.

If you decide to fish a floating/diving bait, always let it settle into the surface film before beginning your retrieve. Often, a really nice panfish will be nearby and will drift over and simply inhale your lure as it's jiggling on the top, rings from its splashdown settling around it.

And let's say you're fishing for crappies and other panfish using ultralight crankbaits and, for some reason, you just can't buy a bite. Try ripping your lure through the water using as fast a retrieve as you can without totally ruining the bait's inherent action.

You'll take all kinds of crappies and nice green sunfish by barely letting the little plug hit the water before you start reeling it in as fast as you can. Maybe the fish react to what they see as a fleeing meal. For whatever the reason, they'll strike on cast after cast.

Beginner's Bait Box

If I were just starting out on this ultralight journey, here's what I'd put together in a crankbait box for panfish:

- Some small **crawdad imitations**, mostly in natural colors.
- Some **minnow baits** in natural colors and in fire tiger, which is a bright combination that includes shades of chartreuse, orange and yellow.
- At least a few **topwater poppers** in shiny colors like silver and gold.
- Some small **lipless crankbaits**, again in those shiny colors.

Let's say I put that box together over the winter, during the off-season for many anglers who either don't enjoy or don't have access to ice fishing, or who prefer to spend their winter months outdoors hunting instead of fishing. Once assembled, I put that box up and write a note to myself to retrieve it sometime around the middle of April, depending on where I live.

In the southern U.S., I could probably start catching crappies and panfish on lures from that box a few weeks earlier. And up North, it might be a few weeks later. But from the time spring sunshine started warming the places I fished until falling leaves began blowing across the water in September or October, I could take just that box, if I chose to, and know I could catch crappies and panfish on virtually every outing.

Spoons

If there's any bait that gets less respect than a crankbait when it comes to fishing ultralight gear for crappies and panfish, it has to be a spoon. Really—have you ever tried one with the idea of catching a big crappie on it?

Maybe you have in winter, through a hole in the ice. But I'm not talking about jigging spoons here. Rather, I'm suggesting that you think about using ultralight-size versions of Dardevles and Johnson Silver Minnows.

The latter might just be the best bet of all when you encounter an area that looks terribly fishy—precisely because it's choked with aquatic vegetation. There are few lures you can use to effectively fish cover like this that work as well as the virtually weedless Silver Minnow. And it's available in sizes as small as 1/24 ounce (1.2 g), making it an ultralight choice to keep in mind.

Dardevles, in their smallest size, come equipped with a double hook instead of a treble. The lack of a third hook point doesn't diminish the potency of this diminutive spoon, and it's available in a bunch of colors that panfish seem to love.

The old standby red-and-white works well. So does silver, silver and blue, yellow; honestly, it will be tougher to find a color combination the fish won't hit. One of the most attractive elements of fishing for crappies and panfish with ultralight gear, especially with spoons, is that the fish seem to respond more to the baits' action than to their colors. And make no mistake; those reactions are often vicious!

One very effective method for spoon-feeding crappies and panfish is to use a stop-and-go retrieve that causes the lures to swim erratically when you crank the reel, then flutter down several inches when you pause. I've most often had crappies or big bluegills bite either during the pause, or just after I start cranking again.

When they hit that way, I can just imagine them under the surface, attracted to the bait by its action, then stopping when it stops, watching it flutter down right across their noses. Then, all at once, it jerks away from them! I don't think they know what else to do but inhale it.

Location Is the Key

With all of these baits, location is a critical factor. As mentioned earlier, there are going to be spots on your favorite waters that just seem to attract crappies and panfish like magnets. These are the places to go for lots of action on a regular basis.

Just don't get discouraged if you consistently take only small- to average-size crappies, bluegills and sunfish from these areas. The largest available panfish in any given fishery are going to act the most predatory. Although there are some lakes, for example, where management and fishing pressure have combined to produce crappie fisheries with outstanding average size, most 2-pound (0.9-kg) crappies and 1-pound (0.45-kg) sunfish don't grow to that size without developing the keenest of predator ways.

These are the fish you'll have to hunt, but they're also the fish that respond most aggressively to any of the ultralight lures and methods you care to try. And there's one other element of your search for trophies that can improve your odds significantly over time: Remember where and how you encountered the large fish.

Take the time to think about the time of year, time of day, weather patterns; they all will help you start developing a pattern approach to your ultralight panfishing.

That big black crappie mentioned near the beginning of this chapter's section on crankbaits wasn't the only big ol' slabside I took from that spot using that technique. It simply was the first.

On later trips to that lake, I knew that there was some kind of feature along that steep, rocky shoreline that attracted and held at least one large crappie. My approach, then, simply involved always taking the time to fish that spot thoroughly. I started out with the crankbaits or a spinner— something that would trigger a response strike from a fish as the lure moved by it. If that didn't work, I took the time to slow down and use a jig, or maybe let a spoon flutter down that drop-off.

On more than one occasion, other fish bit there. Most often, they were other black crappies. But now and again, a keeper largemouth would be there. There were never a lot of fish in that specific area; but there always were some, and they always were a nice size.

So just like those spots that hold schools of panfish, there will be those places where the big ones go to hang out and look for easy prey to ambush.

Chapter 6
Pike and Muskies

Big, toothy fish have always fascinated me. For this then-young angler, the mystery of pike and muskies lurked on the ridges east of my home, which straddled US40 near Pennsylvania's border with Maryland and the Youghiogheny Reservoir. It impounds a river that actually heads up in Preston County, West Virginia; tumbles north through a mix of mountain valleys and meadows in Garrett County, Maryland; then slows down and forms a lake that offers anglers a chance at trophy fish with sharp teeth.

Trout also live there, and my trips to the reservoir always were focused on them. But there was this little part of me that wondered, half excited and half afraid, what would happen if a big ol' pike came along and picked up my bottom-fished bait. On the ultralight gear I had already come to prefer, I knew the fight would be interesting, albeit likely short-lived and fruitless. How can you tame those toothy monsters with such light tackle?

Over the years, I've learned that it's not that tough—although I'm not going to suggest that you head out with a 5-foot (1.5-m), whippy-action UL spinning rod; a tiny open-face reel spooled with 4-pound (1.8-kg) line; and a handful of little baits with even littler treble hooks.

When it comes to pike and muskies, ultralight becomes a relative term. This is one of the chapters in this book where our 1/4-ounce (7-g) weight limit goes out the window—at least partially. For the most part, ultralight fishing for these leviathans involves using heavier tackle, heavier line and heavier lures than for any other species covered in this book. That, however, doesn't mean that it will be any less challenging, especially if you focus on muskies. They are, without question, the most mysterious fish I've ever chased.

For me, at least, pike have always been more about ruthless aggression and fiery action. They are, in many ways, predictable.

Muskies, on the other hand, are like the central characters in the most twisted of suspense novels. If you ever spend time fishing just for them, you understand. You already know to laugh at anglers who say they have them all figured out. Nobody does; and that's what makes them so appealing to me. They are, regardless of the tackle, baits and techniques you use, the most challenging of the freshwater gamefish species I've chased.

If I were going to make a general suggestion to an angler reading this book who'd never fished for either species, I'd point him or her in the direction of pike first because they are going to offer more potential for success more often. I'd suggest using them to learn how both of these fish react and how they bite; how to play and land them; handle and release them.

Then go after muskies. Some will disagree but, for me, pike fishing is like AAA baseball, and muskie fishing is "The Show!" Once you've tried it, you can't get it out of your system. At least, I can't.

That's why this book on angling the ultralight way simply had to include a chapter on adapting these concepts to pike and muskies. The tackle and lures are different than practically anything else you'll read about in these pages, but the mindset is the same. If you subscribe to what follows, you're going to give yourself the chance to enjoy more fishing fun and action—and challenge—than just about anything you've ever tried on the water.

I think this chapter is especially important for those of you who take fishing vacations to the traditional pike and muskie haunts found in Canada, Minnesota and Wisconsin. Many of the waters you visit offer good angling for other species, too, such as smallmouth bass, panfish and walleyes. Taking this ultralight approach to the big, toothy variety you encounter helps you to be able to pack less gear while enjoying the fishing more.

Tackle

Think about this as we start considering "ultralight" tackle for pike and muskies: A "fingerling" muskie is 18 inches (45 cm) long. At least, they are in Missouri, where the state Department of Conservation has managed Lake Pomme de Terre as a muskie fishery for more than thirty-five years. It's a 7,500-acre (3,000-hectare) impoundment tucked between Truman Lake and Lake of the Ozarks.

Trout fingerlings are, what, maybe 3 to 4 inches (7.6 to 10 cm)? Bass and walleye fingerlings about the same? So, we're talking about lightening up for fish that, you can argue, are more than four times as large as most of the other species covered in this book.

That doesn't mean I'm going to cut you that much slack when it comes to tackle! Here, going ultralight for pike and muskies means using line no heavier than 10-pound-test (4.5-kg) and considering rods and reels that are balanced to handle that line weight.

Rods

Setting a weight limit of 10-pound-test (4.5-kg) goes a long way toward determining the rods you can use for this kind of angling action. Making the final choice will depend on just how light you want to go.

For the lightest approach you can take, you'll have to stick with spinning gear because there just aren't too many light-action baitcasting rods on the market. I've always considered that a shame because there's a lot of fishing fun going untapped because baitcasting fans don't have many options if they want to lighten up.

For example, Shakespeare's moderately priced and hugely popular Ugly Stik line of rods includes only one model rated medium-light; and it handles line from 8 to 20 pounds (3.6 to 9 kg) and lures up to 3/4 ounce (21 g).

Some higher-priced lines (G.Loomis, for example) offer several models of casting rods that are balanced to handle 6- to 12-pound-test (2.7- to 5.4-kg) line. That's the kind of casting rod I want to go ultralight pike

Shakespeare Ugly Stik Freshwater 7', 2-piece medium-light rod

St. Croix Premier line of casting rods offers several choices in the 5' 6" to 7' range with fast action using 10-pound-test line.

PIKE AND MUSKIES

and muskie fishing. Just know that most models in that power range are going to cost you a lot more than the 7-foot (2.1-m) Ugly Stik mentioned above.

Spinning rods are another story altogether. You should be able to find one that's perfect for the 10-pound (4.5-kg) line we've settled on here in just about any price range. All of the manufacturers have quality products. Just take your time to choose the rod that feels the best to you. I believe that's an important consideration, and one that is often overlooked.

Because there are so many spinning rods in this power range, you are going to get a lot of different feels, or actions, in rods. Some will be soft, which means the blank will flex throughout much of its length. On the opposite end are the fast-action or extremely fast action rods, which flex only at the very top and provide exceptional power—especially for hook-setting. Moderate-action rods are in the middle, and comprise the widest selection of models from various manufacturers. Fast-action rods tend to be the more expensive, but

there are bargains out there.

I've found real buys in models from St. Croix and Rapala that offer the fast action I prefer. There are those who, no doubt, will argue that a softer rod is better for pike and muskies because these fish are generally going to be hitting moving lures and have hard mouths. Their logic is that the rod flex will enhance your ability to apply power to what I think of as a dynamic hook-set—that is, one that has to happen as the lure and fish continue to move together.

My take is a little different. I spend time sharpening the hooks on my baits in advance of a pike or muskie outing, even if those baits are just out of the package. Razor-sharp hooks are a must for these fish. And when they hit baits equipped with those finely honed points, I want the kind of rod that will apply pressure to them immediately and keep it on without even the slightest hint of give.

Admittedly, that's what I'm used to. One of the reasons I delved into alternatives to truly UL outfits in the earlier chapter on tackle is that I don't care

much for rods that feel wimpy or too whippy. Give me a faster-action rod balanced for UL lines and lures, and I take it every time.

For pike and muskies, any rod that is balanced for 10-pound (4.5-kg) line and that feels good to you will work. Just remember that longer rods generally provide the ability to make longer casts, and that can be helpful when you're fishing big bays on lakes and reservoirs, and you want to cover as much water as possible with every cast.

For that reason, try to choose rods at least 6 feet (1.8 m) long. You'll find some in the 6 1/2- to 7-foot (1.9- to 2.1-m) range that are light enough for UL pike and muskies, and they will be optimum choices.

Having said all that, here is another UL option that will be all kinds of fun, especially when long casts are not important (such as river fishing): Go with a 5 1/2-foot (1.7-m) medium-action bass rod; a baitcaster. You'll find them in this length range that are balanced to handle 8- to 17-pound or 8- to 20-pound (3.6- to 7.6-kg or 3.6- to 9-kg) lines, with usually moderately fast actions.

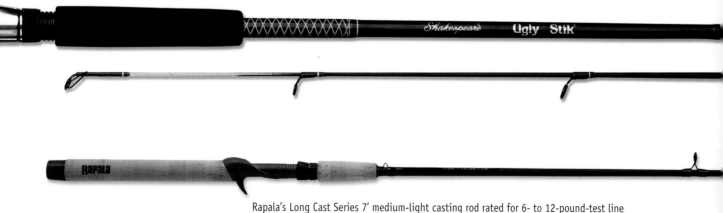

Rapala's Long Cast Series 7' medium-light casting rod rated for 6- to 12-pound-test line

Reels

There are more quality fishing reels available today than at just about any other time in history. When you get around to choosing ones you'll use for this type of ultralight fishing, I believe your key concerns will be line capacity and retrieve speed.

Pick a baitcasting or spinning reel that will handle at least 100 yards (91 m) of 10-pound (4.5-kg) line. And 150 yards (136 m) is better. Reels of this size offer enough line capacity to let a big fish make a run without having to put on a lot of initial pressure, and their dimensions and weight will provide a very comfortable balance.

You'll end up with the kind of outfit you'll not get tired of holding and using, which is important because you're often going to make tons of casts between fish—especially when you're after muskies.

Retrieve speed is important because it seems you can't fish fast enough at certain times of the fishing season on pike and muskie waters. You can always slow down your retrieve, but you can't make a reel work faster than its retrieve rate will allow.

In baitcasters, my No. 1 choice would have to be Daiwa's Procaster PT33SH, for a couple of reasons. Its 7:1 retrieve ratio is the quickest you'll find, and this particular model has been in Daiwa's line for years. It's a tried-and-true design, and with five ball bearings in the drive, it's smooth and pretty rugged.

Honestly, however, all but the very least expensive reels you might select will be built to handle pike and muskies, vicious as they can be. Once again, as with lines, technology has led to improvements in reel design and construction that make today's crop the best ever.

You won't go wrong if you follow these simple steps in picking reels: (1) Stick with the brands you know; (2) go for the fastest retrieve rates you can find; (3) make sure the reels will handle at least 100 yards (91 m) of 10-pound (4.5-kg) line.

Lines

Fishing line technology has advanced to the point where anglers who choose to take the ultralight route to pike and muskie heaven have a better chance of actually getting there than at any other time in modern angling history.

Monofilament is better than ever these days, but it's almost like an annoyance when it comes to line that can handle 3 to 4 feet (0.9 to 1.2 m) of cantankerous fish that includes a mouthful of razor-sharp chompers. You have so many choices

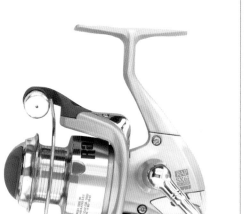

Rapala SX6i spinning reel

Bass-size baitcasting and spinning reels are perfect for a UL pike or muskie rig. They will provide years of service and are rugged enough to handle these big toothy critters, while giving you the excitement of UL-style action.

Daiwa Procaster PT33SH

Berkley Big Game
monofilament line

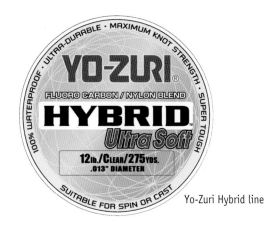

Yo-Zuri Hybrid line

in line types alone, it's amazing. (Please note that every line mentioned in the following paragraphs is available in 10-pound-test/4.5-kg.)

You can go the mono route, for example, with a line like Berkley's Big Game, which is touted as offering the best of abrasion and shock resistance. I know from personal experience that similar qualities are found in monofilament lines from Stren, Maxima, P-Line, and the house brands from Bass Pro Shops and Cabela's.

For the past decade or so, the "hot" fishing lines have been the new high-tech braids like Spiderwire. They're smaller in diameter than the traditional Dacron braided lines that have been around forever, permitting them to offer superior strength in a given line diameter.

More recently, even more new technology has found its way to fishing lines. You can buy spectra line, fluorocarbon line and hybrid line that combines monofilament and fluorocarbon. All of them provide more strength than any line could when I first started fishing for pike and muskies.

My line recommendations are simple: If you want to take a traditional route, go with one of today's advanced braids. For generations, dyed-in-the-wool pike and muskie anglers swore by the old-time braid because it didn't stretch and offered strength they could count on. Today's super braids are all of that, and more.

If, on the other hand, you want to get out there on the edge, opt for a fluorocarbon or hybrid line. In a given line weight, they are stronger than any non-braid ever brought to the fishing tackle shelves of your favorite store.

Curiosity led me to try one of these new lines, and I opted for Yo-Zuri's monofilament-fluorocarbon hybrid, in 6-pound-test (2.7-kg). Spooling it on one of my favorite spinning outfits for trout, I wondered how it would be in terms of knot strength and abrasion resistance.

It's just fine in those areas, and even stronger than I ever imagined 6-pound line could be. On at least four different occasions during the first month I used the stuff, I pulled and yanked on ¼-ounce (7-g)

inline spinners that I snagged in rocks or sunken tree limbs until the lures came free—because the hook that had been stuck straightened out! I've never before been able to put so much stress on 6-pound line that my hook straightened before the line broke. Doing it once might have been luck; four times is proof that these new lines are something else.

I prefer these lines over the new superbraids primarily because you can get them in clear or shaded versions that give me more confidence because they don't appear to be so visible. Line visibility probably hasn't ever stopped a big pike or muskie from striking, but the visibility, or lack of it, is something that matters to me.

Regardless of which way you go—superbraid or high-tech non-braided line—your 10-pound-test (4.5-kg) line will give you a fighting, ultralight chance at a big pike or muskie. Just take the time to adjust your reel's drag properly so that a big fish doesn't shock the line, and you, with a surprise turn or bullish run.

Lures

I caught my first muskie on a huge wooden jerkbait, a Suick, that looks a lot like a hunk of broom handle, painted black, with big treble hooks. It was so heavy that I needed what amounted to a saltwater bait-casting outfit, and it plum wore me out.

I like fishing for muskies; but going the ultralight route described in this chapter allows me to do it with more fun and less work. When it comes to baits, I guess you could say that I go bass fishing for pike and muskies.

Many of the lures you'll read about here are more well known for taking largemouths than they are for taking fish with mouths full of large teeth. But that doesn't make them any less effective on the latter; they're just ultralight alternatives to the bigger, heavier baits that most folks envision when talk turns to pike and muskies.

If there's any drawback to using these baits, you'll find it on fisheries where bass share their hideouts with one or both sharp-toothed species. That is, you're liable to have a perfectly good pike outing "spoiled" when a 5-pound (2.25-kg) bass hits your bait. If that idea really does bother you, maybe you should just stick with the super heavyweight gear.

It never bothers me. Although I fish baits and use presentations in areas where I either know or believe I can run into a pike or muskie, I also know that a big bass might just add a fun diversion to the day.

Soft Plastics

That's especially true when you choose to fish soft-plastic baits. Admittedly, I consider them only for pike because I enjoy fishing other baits for muskies a lot more. But plastics are effective on pike in some situations.

The most vivid example that comes to mind involves submerged weedline on lakes and rivers. These are spots pike just love, and spots where plastics will turn them on.

I learned this first-hand on Gull Lake, just west of Brainerd, Minnesota, more than ten years ago on an outing with the late Leslie Lovett and our mutual close friend, Richard Brady. We were all in the area for the annual visit of the National Hot Rod Association drag races. Lovett was photo editor of

NHRA's weekly newspaper, *National Dragster*; and Brady was—and is—one of NHRA's chief photographers.

They always got to Brainerd a few days early because both of them loved to fish as much as they loved hot rods on quarter-mile (0.4-km) racetracks. I joined them one sultry August for some pre-race fishing. When we headed out that first morning, Brady immediately rigged a 7-inch (18-cm), black plastic worm on one of his bass rods.

Lovett and I were fishing jig-tipped minnows for walleyes along a flooded weedline when Brady got the day's first attention from below. Several minutes later, he boated a 6-pound (2.7-kg) pike that set the tone for the day. His worm fooled fish after fish, teaching me a lot about how pike often eagerly take plastics I only previously considered when bass were the targets.

Brady used the simplest rig of all—a standard, round, 1/4-ounce (7-g) jig head. He threaded the hook into the worm, then finished rigging it like a standard jig, hook point exposed. He picked up grass that way, but wasted no more time as a result than he would have unwrapping the same tangles of vegetation from a Texas-rigged worm that was weedless.

Today, you can even find over-size tube baits, like Lindy's Tiger Tubes—6- and 8-inch (15- and 20-cm) versions of lures that most bass anglers consider finesse baits. That's pretty funny because there's nothing ever finesse-like about pike and muskie fishing!

Quarter-ounce (7-g) weights are about right for nearly any situation you'll encounter on

Yamamoto plastic baits include (top to bottom): 6 1/2" Kut-Tail worm, 5 1/2" Double Tail Hula Grub, 5" Craw and 7" Lizard.

Lindy Tiger Tubes come in 6" and 8" sizes with 3/4-oz. or 5/8-oz. jig head.

this UL pike and muskie journey. Your choices in soft plastics run to larger worms; the big tube baits; large curly-tail grubs; even big creature-style baits like 5-inch (12.7-cm) Hula Grubs.

Although there are plenty of places you can fish them, I generally stick to the kinds of weedy underwater structure described here because in other situations, I opt for other kinds of lures. It's a matter of personal preference as much as anything.

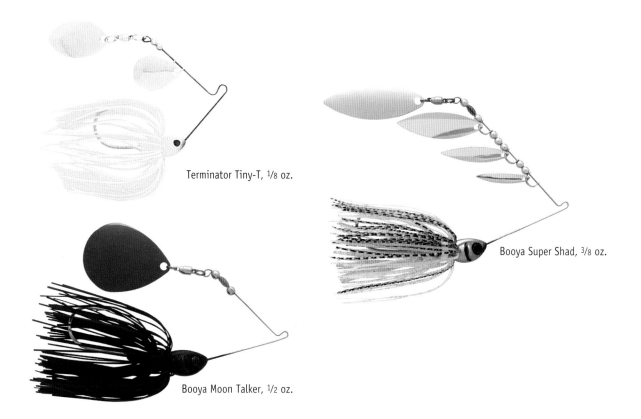

Terminator Tiny-T, 1/8 oz.

Booya Super Shad, 3/8 oz.

Booya Moon Talker, 1/2 oz.

Spinnerbaits

My personal favorite for pike and muskies is a spinnerbait, for a couple of reasons. First, and most important, you can cover a lot of water with them. That can be very important in this game because these large predators are sometimes contrary about how and when they strike—especially muskies. Maybe you've heard them referred to as "the fish of 1,000 casts."

Second, you can definitely take an ultralight approach with spinnerbaits and still present the fish with a large bait profile. As evidence, I offer Hammerin' Hare lures, which feature rabbit-hair skirts and trailers. This line of spinnerbaits, buzzbaits and jigs gets really close to the look you get when casting bucktail spinners that are many times heavier—but not a whole lot larger in silhouette.

You can go as light as 1/4 ounce (7 g) with these lures. If you stepped "all the way up" to a 1/2-ounce (14-g) model, given the lighter rods and reels you're using with 10-pound (4.5-kg) line, you can cover virtually the same amount of water as you could with a telephone pole of a rod and a spinner weighing more than 1 ounce (28 g).

If you've never fished for pike and muskies before, all you'd have to do is hold a traditional heavy outfit in one hand and the UL rig described here in the other to know without question which one you'd enjoy fishing with over a long day on the water.

Something else you'll learn after only an encounter or two with a hefty pike or muskie is that they really tear up your baits with those needle-like teeth. With that in mind, you also should look at the spinnerbaits now on the market that

feature titanium wire in their construction.

When it comes to spinnerbaits, both species seem to react well to lures that disturb a lot of water when you fish them. For that reason, definitely consider using one of the Strike King titanium baits that feature a whopping four spinner blades. The French Quarter Titanium uses French-style blades, while the Original Titanium Quad Shad uses a quartet of willow-leaf blades.

The spinning lures mentioned so far are the safety-pin style that bass anglers know and love. But pike and muskie chasers often opt for heavy, oversize inline models that feature bucktail dressings.

You'll have a hard time finding UL baits like this, but there is a titanium inline option—Terminator's weedless inline, which is rigged with a soft-plastic body in weedless fashion.

You'd probably improve its fish-catching ability for pike and muskies by actually exposing the hook point, but it does provide a useful option if you want to go inline with your spinners.

Safety-pin spinners are my personal preference because, regardless of their size, they always present a bigger profile in the water. I believe that makes a difference to pike and muskies. And for that reason, even with spinnerbaits as small as 1/4 ounce/7 g (you can get those four-bladed Strike King baits that light!), I'm going to add some kind of trailer that will enhance the lure's look and action as it moves through the water.

In this case, bigger is better. I go with an extra-large curly-tail grub, or even a twin-tail. The more action the better because I'm going to be burning these lures on every cast, just under the surface. That's the pike and muskie way when it comes to spinnerbaits.

My color palette for these lures is going to be pretty simple, though. I want baits with black skirts and dressings for bright days—and sometimes even on overcast days—and chartreuse as my alternative. These two shades have worked for me time and time again, so I stick with them.

Buzzbaits

There is another kind of "spinner" you have to keep in mind, especially during the summer months—buzzbaits. Pike absolutely go nuts over them, and muskies sure won't shy away from them!

That day on Minnesota's Gull Lake with Lovett and Brady ended with the three of us casting buzzbaits through lily pads and across the tops of submerged weed beds, and the pike enthusiastically rewarded our efforts. At that time, the only buzzbaits I owned would be considered ultralight even by bass-angling standard—they were only 1/8-ounce (3.5-g) models! But several pike sure didn't mind their light weight—especially the baits with black skirts, and the purple ones.

Buzzbaits are lots of fun to use on pike and muskies because you can find such large ones that don't weigh very much at all. That Hammerin' Hare line mentioned earlier even includes twin-blade buzzbait models that easily weigh in as ultralights for pike and muskies.

OK. So where are you going to fish all these bladed baits? On lakes; it's hard to beat them on flats that have weed beds or other kinds of structure.

For example, on Pomme de Terre in Missouri, one of the most consistently productive muskie spots in the whole fishery is a long flat, nothing more than a flooded stump bed. It's never more than about 6 to 7 feet (1.8 to 2.1 m) deep from the shore out more than 100 yards (91 m). If there's a textbook hotspot for fishing spinnerbaits and buzzbaits for pike and muskies, this is it. On northern lakes, those stumps might be replaced by flooded weeds, or mixed with them. Either way, flats (including shallow bays and coves) are prime areas to cover with these lures.

On rivers, you'll find similar areas—sandbars and eddies. But spinnerbaits and buzzbaits also are great lures to use in probing shoreline cover like trees that have fallen into the water. This really is a lot like bass fishing; the only difference is, you're on fisheries that also are home to big fish with big teeth. My rule of thumb for fishing any of these locations is pretty simple: If I consistently fish a given area or stretch of riverbank without ever catching a bass—and I know there are bass in the fishery—then I believe it's reasonable to conclude that I'm fishing over pike or muskies. Sometimes, they show themselves; other times, especially with muskies, they won't. But the lack of attention from bass when fishing these baits these ways actually gives me confidence that I'm in the right spots for the bigger fish I'm after.

Booya Buzz, 1/4 oz.

Rapala Husky Jerk, 5½", ½ oz.

Bill Lewis Slap-Stick, ³⁄₈ oz.

Rebel Jointed Minnow, 5½", ¹¹⁄₁₆ oz.

Lindy 4½" Gator Spoon

Crankbaits

Forget about the Suicks and big Drifter Tackle Believers. For novice pike and muskie anglers, these are the names of some well-known and very effective lures that are large, heavy and, as a result, tiresome to fish.

We're talking ultralight here. And for pike and muskies, that means bass lures—and primarily, it means stickbaits like Rapalas, Rebels and Bombers. And don't think for a minute that these lures won't work in place of those XXL lures mentioned above. They do.

Here, I'm talking about baits that are 6 to 7 inches (15 to 18 cm) long, either jointed or one-piece. In most cases, I opt for the jointed lures because I can fish them in ways that will impart more action—and action draws attention from pike and muskies.

One example is to fish a broken-back Rebel, a jointed stickbait, with a fast, herky-jerky retrieve. Its wounded-looking ways often entice big fish to at least come up for a look. Pike often go ahead and hit it. Muskies can be more finicky.

Some days, however, the fish won't be too picky. All you may have to do to entice a strike is figure out the most attractive way to retrieve your crankbait or, at most, switch from a jointed to a one-piece model. The latter is especially effective, using what I call a traditional jerkbait retrieve.

You cast the lure, crank your reel several times to get the lure down to its standard working depth (usually no more than 4 feet/1.2 m with a floating/diving model) then begin sweeping your rod to move the bait. Point the rod tip at the lure, at about 10 o'clock, then sweep it down and toward you. Or, you can point it straight out and sweep to one side or the other. When you finish a sweep, crank in your slack line as you return the rod tip to the starting position, then sweep again. Repeat this all the way to the boat.

Often, fish hit the bait during the pause between sweeps. You sweep, stop and crank; sweep, stop and crank. Then, try to sweep again, only to feel several pounds of mean fish tugging at the end of your line.

For a twist to this approach, take a floating/diving stickbait, and add some weight to it using either lead golf tape, which is used to adjust the swing weight of clubs, or the commercially available adhesive weights some fishing lure makers, such as Storm, sell. Do this weight thing at home, with water in a sink or

You can put lead tape on stickbaits to make them neutrally buoyant and hover at the same depth they normally run at.

tub, so you can test the lure's buoyancy.

You want it to be as close as possible to neutral buoyancy—when you push the lure down, under the surface, it stops almost completely motionless. This is a tactic that bass anglers have been using for the past decade or so during the pre-spawn, with amazing results.

Now, the traditional thinking in the pike and muskie world is that jerkbaits trigger a strike response during the pause because they slowly begin floating toward the surface during that pause, as you're reeling in slack. That may be true, but it doesn't always work. Taking this approach to adding weight simply gives your bait another, different look, and that, too, can trigger strikes.

And here's a little secret: There is a stickbait on the market that, when weighted, will give you the best of both worlds—it will move, but won't change its depth if you have it weighted properly. Louisiana-based Bill Lewis Lures, which makes the popular Rat-L-Trap lipless crankbait, makes it; it's called a Slap-Stick.

And it's different because every lure has a chamber that holds a few small shot. When you retrieve the lure, either steadily or with a jerk, it moves through the water horizontally. But when you pause, gravity causes those shot to move to the bottom of the chamber, and that movement causes the tail of the lure to drop. So at rest, Slap-Sticks sit in the surface film nose-up. When you weight them to reach neutral buoyancy, they do the same thing—but at their standard running depth!

Imagine a bait you could move through the water a few feet (meters) deep, just under a pike or muskie, then pause and have it slowly change position while it remains at the same depth. It's a look these fish haven't seen very often, if at all, and it's guaranteed to trigger some strikes for you.

Any of these lures are especially effective when fished parallel to (1) the edges of weed-lines; (2) structure breaks (like where a flat drops into deeper water); (3) a main or secondary point; and (4) areas where structure or bottom type changes from, say, rocks to wood. Again, if you're a bass angler, this is the kind of approach you'd use with the lures if you were after largemouths. It's the same principle; just different, larger, meaner fish!

Spoons

I feel obligated to include spoons in this chapter because they are such effective baits on pike and muskies. The problem is that their design inherently makes it difficult to recommend ultralight options. Spoons that work best on these fish present fairly large profiles; and the only spoons with large profiles are, themselves, large and, as a result, heavy.

Companies like Dardevle, Mepps, Luhr-Jensen and Bomber do, however, make versions of their spoons in the 3-inch (7.6-cm) range that weigh between 3/8 and 5.8 ounces (10.6 and 164 g). These are not the best choices in lures for pike and muskies because they're not very large; but if you want to give this ultralight approach a try and you want to fish spoons, they are your best choices.

Chapter 7
Catfish

Catfish offer you the best opportunity to hook, play and land really large trophies on the lightest fishing tackle you can use. If you like the thought of wrestling with 10-, 15-, 20-pound (4.5-, 6.75-, 9-kg) or heavier fish on the kind of rods, reels and lines most anglers would only consider for bluegills or brook trout, then read on.

Tackle

Use whatever you want, as light as you want it. My logic is simple: Most often, catfishing with a rod and reel involves still-fishing. Usually, you are casting a live or prepared bait from the bank or from your boat and waiting for the fish to show up hungry.

Catfish will hit artificial baits like spinners and plugs. But day in and day out, the best way to catch them is to fish some kind of natural bait on or just off the bottom.

Rods

You could accomplish that with a 4½-foot (1.4-m) ultralight rod and a tiny reel spooled with 2-pound-test (0.9-kg) line. But if you're on a fishery with big cats like flatheads, that really is a losing proposition.

On a farm pond stocked with channel cats that range up to 5 pounds (2.25 kg) or so, that kind of outfit would be a lot of fun to fish with. But this section is about trophy cats, the biggest of the big. And for them, ultralight tackle is just a little bit bigger. It still falls within my guidelines. But I suggest you stick with 6-pound (2.7-kg) line, and that you definitely use a rod at least 6 feet (1.8 m) long because doing so will help you to make longer casts—and they often are necessary when fishing from the shore.

On rivers, where you also have to take the current into consideration, a long rod is the way to go because, admittedly, you'll likely have to break the rule of balance when it comes to the amount of weight you use to keep your bait in the strike zone.

If you're using an ultralight outfit and 6-pound (2.7-kg) line, but you have to add an ounce (28 g) of weight to keep your bait down, that rig is going to be a handful to cast. It's the most significant tackle consideration in this chapter because it affects your ability to cast accurately and for distance. Long rods make it easier to lob that kind of offering out where it needs to be, which gives you a chance to play heavyweights on lightweight rigs.

Reels

The next most significant tackle consideration is your drag. It's not easy to turn even a 10-pound (4.5-kg) catfish on a heavy-action outfit; so imagine what it will be like with a UL rod and reel. You must take the time to set your drag so that fish will feel some pressure, but still can gain some line from you if necessary.

Speaking of gaining line, the next most significant tackle consideration is the capacity of the reel you're using. Don't settle for anything less than at least 100 yards (91 m) of whatever line size you plan to use. Because today's lines are stronger yet thinner than any before them, I recommend that you even consider using my standard UL reel model, which accepts 100 yards of 6-pound (2.7-kg) line; but spool it with 4-pound (1.8-kg) superline of some type. You'll gain some capacity this way, and still be walking on the good side of the conversation about line strength versus fighting ability of the fish.

Baits for catfish include bluegill (top left), gizzard shad (top right), golden shiner (middle left), skipjack herring (middle right) and carp (bottom left).

Bait

If you get your bait from a tackle shop or local bait house, use large goldfish if they have them because big cats love them. Some anglers might cringe at that thought, and suggest that if a goldfish gets into a pond or river system that doesn't already have them, you run the risk of introducing a species of rough fish that could explode in numbers and damage your water. If you agree that's a concern, fish dead-bait rigs. Cats seem to react much more positively to live bait, but they also seem to really go for goldfish—dead or alive.

Large minnows or shiners also work, but you generally won't be able to buy them as big as you can goldfish. And if channel cats are your primary targets, you can even use nightcrawlers or chunks of hot dog with good success. And don't think a piece of hot dog from the grocery store won't entice a big channel cat to bite—it definitely will. That's probably the best bait to use if you've got youngsters along because the bait won't bother them. In fact, it'll probably tickle them to think about cats looking for hot dogs on the bottom of the lake or river.

Where to Fish

My perfect catfish location on a lake or river is one that gives me access to shallow and deep water from the same spot. Elsewhere in this book, I mention a 250-acre (100-hectare) public lake in eastern Kansas that I fished regularly over more than nine angling seasons. It had just such a spot, which was almost textbook perfect.

Lake Olathe had a cove on its east shoreline, and the mouth of that cove dropped from about 8 to 10 feet (2.4 to 3 m) down to more than 30 feet (9 m) in less than 60 feet (18 m).

From the shore, just inside the cove, I could cast one bait into the deep water, or maybe just at the edge of the drop. I could cast another out into the cove or just along its edge, where the water was 6 feet (1.8 m) deep or shallower.

Catfish can be wanderers and they often move from deep water to shallow to feed. I remember being in a float tube, bass fishing the shoreline cover in that cove one early evening, when I noticed what I at first thought was a wad of baitfish just under the surface about 40 feet (12 m) in front of me. I was just about to cast the little crankbait I was using into the middle of that bait when I realized it wasn't bait at all, but a flathead catfish more than 3 feet (0.9 m) long!

It was still daylight, and this fish was cruising around just under the surface, undoubtedly looking for some dinner. I learned from this encounter that big cats don't always wait until night falls to start prowling for food; and that this spot was one the lake's big cats were using, and part of the reason had to be its proximity to the deeper water.

Reaching the cove mouth's drop-off with a cast from the shore meant having an outfit that would permit a cast of about 25 to 30 yards (23 to 27 m). When you're using live or prepared bait, that can be a tricky proposition unless you have a long rod. That's why I recommend one of at least 6 feet (1.8 m); a 7-footer (2.1 m) would be even better.

Another prime catfish location on a man-made lake is near one of its main creek channels. This, too, usually involves casts longer than 30 to 40 feet (9 to 12 m) because there are few spots in a given body of water where the channel hugs right up against the shore. And generally, those spots are along bluff banks that are impossible to fish without a boat.

My experience has been that channels meander close to the shore of a given impoundment, but "close" often means only within 40 to 50 yards (36.4 to 45.5 m). Longer rods are the only tools you can use to reach out that far with a live-bait rig—especially if it's an ultralight outfit. You can't really put a lot of power into the cast because UL rods by their very nature don't have a lot of power. But a long rod allows you to make a sweeping lob of a cast that will get your bait out where it needs to be.

You can also find spots that offer access to shallow and deep fishing on rivers; they're generally along sandbars and riffles that feed into deep pools. These spots are really prime for night fishing because, on most rivers that hold big cats, those trophies will hold in the deep water until night falls, then move up to the shallows to feed. They likely move up from time to time during the day, too. So even if you're not big on night fishing, finding a spot that will let you present one bait deep and another shallow is the best bet.

I confess that flathead catfish are my favorite species to fish for because they grow very large and they are every bit as predatory as any bass or pike you'll encounter. My preference for flathead bait is green sunfish or bluegills when I can get them because of two things: (1) catfish use them as one of their primary forage sources, and (2) because using them sets up one of the most unique fishing trips you'll ever experience, especially with ultralight tackle.

Catfish are bottom-feeding scavengers. Flatheads, in particular, are among the most aggressive freshwater predators. They love big sunfish and will ambush and attack them almost recklessly.

Choose reels that have a large capacity for 6- or 8-pound-test line.

Fishing Flatheads

We're going lake fishing, and we're going to be on the water about an hour or so before sunset. We're not bringing a lot of tackle because we don't need to. A couple of rods each will be enough. We're hoping to catch a big flathead on a little rod and reel.

My setup will include what I call a traditional UL outfit and a UL flathead outfit. "Traditional" means a short rod, probably 5 feet (1.5 m) or so, with a UL action and a small spinning reel spooled with 4-pound (1.8-kg) line. For flatheads, I have a light rod at least a foot (30 cm) longer with a reel designed to take at least 100 yards (91 m) of 8-pound (3.6-kg) line; but I have it spooled with 6-pound-test (2.7-kg) so I've got more

capacity to play fish.

My tackle for that rig includes large bait hooks— probably 5/0, but maybe even bigger—that I've honed to razor-sharp points, 1/2-ounce (14-g) egg-shaped slip-sinkers and some barrel swivels. We'll talk about rigging it for flatheads after we catch our bait.

And to do that, I use that little UL rig to fish a tiny crankbait or jig for sunfish. We're going to start off hitting the best shoreline cover, which includes weedlines, brush piles and banks featuring gravel or rocks up to golfball size. We keep the sunfish or bluegills we catch that are at least 4 inches (10 cm) long; I prefer 6 inches (15 cm) or larger. They're going in the boat's live well. If you don't have a boat with a live well, a clean 5-gallon (19-l) bait bucket will do the trick because, in most cases, we can quickly catch more bait if we need to.

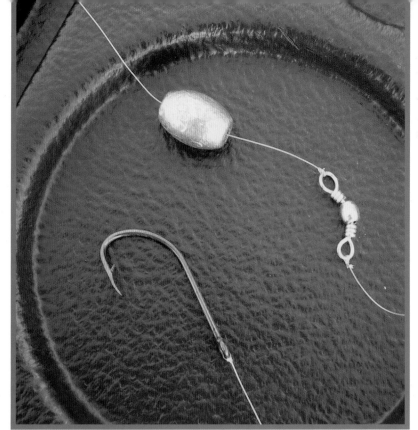

A typical slip-sinker setup for flatheads that gets the bait deep and allows it to swim freely.

So for the hour or so we have until it gets dark, we'll be fishing for panfish; but we'll likely catch a bass here and there, and maybe even some crappies. Those are released because we've got bigger fish to catch later on, and we need to target smaller ones now.

When we've got some scrappy sunfish of the right size, we find a spot near the lake's main channel—one that's adjacent to a flat or near the mouth of a cove. We anchor or tie off there, and get on to the main event by rigging the UL flathead outfit.

I start by cutting a 2- to 3-foot (0.6- to 0.9-m) section of line off the reel and laying it aside; then slide the slip-sinker onto the main line, and tie one end of a barrel swivel to it. Next, I tie one end of that short piece of line to the other end of the barrel swivel, and tie the hook to the other end of the line.

That rig lets the bait move around quite a bit, and at the same time causes it to struggle because it's not strong enough to pull line through the sinker. That combination will draw big flatheads on the prowl.

Next, I hook a sunfish through the back, just below the dorsal fin, or hook it in the tail, just in front of the tail fin. Either will make for quite the feisty bait, creating a commotion at the end of the line.

I cast the rig, using that sweeping-lob of a motion mentioned earlier, to get the bait where I want it. In this case, it's going to be near the deeper water, but not in it. It's getting dark, remember, and the big cats are going to be cruising soon in search of a meal, if they haven't already started.

In my perfect world, there would be baitcasting and spinning reels suitable for use as part of an ultralight rig like this

one that featured a bait-running component—what some anglers commonly know as a clicker. It's like a free-spool setting, except that it provides very slight resistance to keep line from overrunning itself, and it emits an audible click when a fish picks up the bait and starts taking line as it swims away.

In the real world, however, you won't find reels like this. With that in mind, I use a trick from my earliest days of still-fishing: After casting a worm or corn and letting it settle to the bottom, I'd attach a tiny, marble-sized bobber to the line along the rod, between two of the line-guide eyes. I'd pull enough line off the reel to let that bobber droop down a foot (30 cm) or so, and that became my strike indicator. When a fish hit and started off with the bait, the bobber would start rising toward the rod.

Chapter 8
Trout

Trout fishing got me hooked on fishing the ultra-light way more than thirty-five years ago. I was still in grade school then, but with grown-up tastes when it came to the kind of fishing I enjoyed best.

It involved using tiny rods and reels to cast bait or small spinners to hatchery rainbows that were stocked weekly in one of several pothole-size pay-lakes that dotted the landscape near my southwestern Pennsylvania home. Sure, there were trout streams nearby; but I never fished them.

Practically all of the anglers I knew, those of my age as well as adults, preferred the small private ponds to the streams around home. As a novice, I naturally followed their lead. Even my first real fishing rod and reel were adult-sized—a classic Garcia-Mitchell 300 reel on a two-piece St. Croix fiberglass spinning rod.

The whole rig weighed many times what a comparably sized spinning outfit weighs today.

The rod, for example, had metal ferrules; can you imagine?!

But what I remember about that outfit, more than anything else, was its balance. Sure, it was heavier than anything similar you find today. But it truly was balanced, which made it effortless to cast and fish, even for a pre-teen.

Ever since, the concept of balance has been among the most important elements of my tackle shopping, especially for trout gear. No matter which species of gamefish you like to chase best, nothing enhances your enjoyment of fishing like the feel of a perfectly balanced rod and reel.

If there is one kind of action that appears absolutely heaven-sent for UL anglers, it's trout fishing. In fact, I'm willing to bet that when you saw this book's title, your first thought involved trout fishing. Most anglers think like that; they pigeonhole the concept, believing that it applies only to scrappy little trout on small, easy-to-wade streams.

Even UL fanatics can be close-minded like that when it comes to trout fishing. If you're one of them, what follows will help you enjoy more trout, more often, under a variety of conditions on streams of all sizes.

Jigs

Sometimes, especially early in the fishing season, trout chasers who prefer artificial lures will find themselves at a disadvantage if they choose to fish spinners or crankbaits on UL spinning gear rather than opting for nymphs and/or streamers on a flyrod. They cast and cast without success, while fly fishermen nearby are using patterns like wooly buggers or bead-head nymphs to catch all kinds of trout.

If you're one of those non-flyrodders, don't get frustrated; get jigs! They'll get you on track and catching trout just like those guys with flies who often seem to take great delight in out-fishing anglers who use "hardware."

Whenever I think of fishing jigs for trout, I start daydreaming about Missouri's Lake Taneycomo, which flows through Branson, in the Ozarks. Although it's called a lake, Taneycomo really is about an 18-mile (29-km) stretch of the White River.

When I first heard about it, in the early 1980s, Missouri's Department of Conservation was stocking upwards of 90,000 rainbow trout per month in Taneycomo, year-round! Add to

Lindy's Little Nipper, Little Guppy and Quiver jigs that can be used for trout, come in sizes from 1/64 oz. to 1/16 oz.

that a management plan that provided for development of a trophy brown trout fishery, and Taneycomo suddenly starts looking like the really dynamic fishery it is.

I was terribly excited about fishing there; then, I heard more about the tackle and tactics many anglers used. They fished the tiniest of jigs—you might call them microjigs—that varied in weight from 1/64 ounce (0.4 g) at the heaviest down to 1/100 ounce (0.3 g). To get jigs that small to have any realistic action, anglers used 2-pound (0.9-kg) line. Talk about ultralight fishing! But it worked; and it still works.

Your approach is going to be a lot like that of the flyrodders mentioned earlier; you just won't be false-casting or using traditional flies. Instead, you'll be using UL spinning gear and the lightest of lines to fish tiny jigs the way flyrodders fish nymphs—that is, with pretty much a dead-drift presentation.

Jigs have come a long way in the past twenty years, but small maribou-dressed offerings are still about the best you can use for this kind of angling. Unless you live in a part of the country where trout fishing rules, you'll probably have to shop for the smallest crappie jigs you can find. Or, you can tie your own.

A Good Setup

Here's the recipe for the most basic of trout jigs—and one that you can fish on line heavier than 2-pound-test (0.9-kg) with success: You need a few Aberdeen hooks, some split shot and some yarn.

Heck, you can even take a "system" approach to these lures by using removable split-shot—the kind with the little bumps on the back side that permit quick removal. Doing that will give you a way to fine-tune every jig by going to heavier or lighter weight depending on water conditions. I'm still amazed at how effective something so simple can be on a trout stream.

Maybe you still want to go with something that looks better to you, even if the fish don't seem to care much for appearances. If you want to tie your own jigs, you can readily find jig heads of 1/16, 1/32 and even 1/64 ounce (1.7, 0.9, 0.4 g). You can use maribou or synthetic materials used in nymphs and streamers to fashion bodies. Or you can just buy your jigs. Plenty of styles in those lightest of sizes are commercially available.

The most important consideration is color. White definitely works. Brown and black will work, too. If you don't believe that, ask any of the anglers you know what colors of Wooly Bugger they fish more than any others. Olive green also is effective. And if you're going to tie your own jigs, invest the time and money necessary to visit a local fly shop or a Web site that sells tying materials, and get some peacock hurl. There is something about its look that trout just love.

In fact, if you want to stick with the darker shades, a good way to come up with an effective selection of jigs in a hurry is to take a kind of "match the hatch" approach. Either buy or tie jigs that resemble some of the most popular nymph patterns in color and appearance.

Fishing jigs for trout is as simple as fishing live bait or,

Whatever works!

Just a few years ago, I stood about 25 yards (23 m) downstream from an angler probing a fairly deep riffle on Glady Fork, a typical eastern freestone flowage in Randolph County, West Virginia. Most anglers who fish it just call it Glady, and they show up often throughout the late winter and early spring because the Mountain State's Division of Natural Resources stocks Glady weekly each year from March through May.

I was fishing a spinner with hit-and-miss success, but the angler I was fishing upstream toward seemed to be taking trout on about every cast. He was making short, flipping-motion casts to the head of the riffle, and letting his lure drift and tumble downstream with the current. From several feet (meters) away, I could even detect the strikes he was getting because his line would suddenly stop, then move slightly to one side as another hatchery rainbow picked up the bait and turned with it.

Tied onto the end of what looked and felt like 6-pound (2.7-kg) line was a gold Aberdeen hook, about a size 8. There was a split-shot crimped over the shaft of the hook, just below the eye the line was tied to; and there were a couple of strips of white yarn wrapped and tied haphazardly below the split-shot.

for flyrodders, using nymphs and Wooly Buggers. You simply cast them upstream and, controlling your slack line, allow the lure to tumble back toward you as naturally as possible on prevailing currents.

Strikes will vary. The most aggressive of trout will hit so hard they'll pretty much hook themselves. By the time you feel the strike and react, the fight will already be on.

Most fish, however, won't hit like that. They'll simply pick up the bait with a quick move from their ambush holding lie. Your line will just stop; or, you'll see it twitch slightly. Set the hook.

Those three words, in fact, are the most important of all when it comes to jig fishing. When you know you have a strike, set the hook. When you think you have a strike, set the hook. When in doubt, set the hook. You're going to discover that you're snagged fairly often—but you'll also begin to learn that what you thought was a rock or stick getting in the way of your drifting jig actually was a nice trout.

Where to Fish

If you've never fished jigs for trout, ask your fly fishing buddies about the kinds of water where they prefer nymphs over any other kind of artificial. You're going to hear words like "run," "riffle" and "pocket water." These terms all describe stretches of stream or river that are usually thigh deep or shallower and feature plenty of rocks or boulders. These are areas where trout can lie in ambush along the edges of the current and dart out to attack easy meals that drift by.

A key to success when fishing areas like these involves taking as thorough an approach as possible. Do your best to make presentations that will let your jig drift along every current tongue there is in a given stretch. Fish both sides of rocks. Fish across the stream, from one side to the other. One of the best things about fishing this kind of water this way is that you'll find plenty of places holding trout.

That being said, it's tough to

argue that pools remain the most popular spots on any stream, and for good reason. They're deep, and usually have at least average fish-holding cover. These are the places that hold the biggest trout in a given fishery, and the places where jigs can be more successful than many anglers realize.

The reason for that is simple: Most anglers just never think of using a jig when they come to a pool. They fish spinners or crankbaits; or maybe they switch to a natural offering like a worm or minnow. Jigs, if they're on an angler's list of pool options at all, are always near the bottom.

They shouldn't be. You can fish a pool as effectively with a jig as you can with any other bait you might select. Here's how to do it:

Start from the bottom and fish upstream. Begin with casts that let you cover the lower end of the pool with a dead drift. In some cases, you'll be fishing water with little current, so you may have to use a very slow, steady retrieve of your own to cover the slack water on either side of the main current. But, especially early in the morning, trout are often out in that slack, shallower water. If you don't fish it before moving farther up the stream, you run the risk of spooking fish before they ever have a chance to bite. So take the time to fish the lower end of any pool as completely as you can before moving upstream.

You'll likely complete this while standing either in the stream or along the shore, but below the pool. Only after you've fished that bottom section thoroughly should you

Jigs are easy to use in streams; simply cast upstream and allow it to float along in the current, while controlling the slack line. Set the hook whenever it stops—it could be a fish.

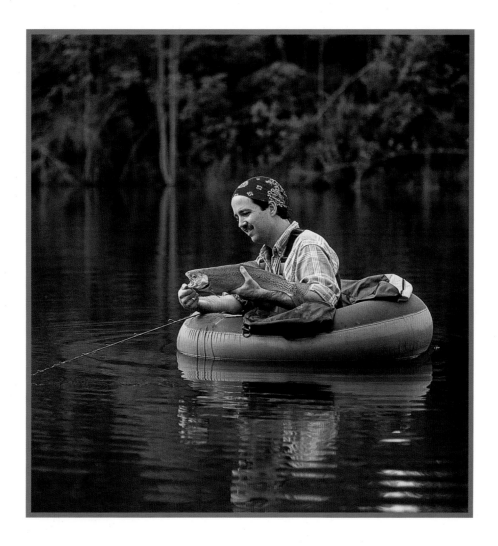

move up into it. Then, shift your attention to the middle section of the pool. Dead drifts are the best presentations here, too. However, you also can begin to use an across-and-down presentation to cover water opposite of where you're standing.

To some, that sounds funny because it suggests covering water again that you've already fished. All I can tell you is that trout often only react to a bait that comes past their holding lie in a certain way, from a certain direction. You should approach every possible fish-holding spot as if it actually does have a trout there, and give that fish every "look" you

can before moving on.

When you can make a cast that reaches the head of the pool, get your jig into the very top of it; let it drift down and into the deeper water with the swiftest part of the current, as if it's a natural morsel tumbling into the deep water from the riffle or run above. You might be surprised by a fish holding just off that fast-moving water. It will dart out and strike in a hurry.

Some pools have rocks at their heads, which will split incoming water into two or three current tongues. Fish them all. I have taken multiple trout from the same pool simply by recognizing that there

could be one holding off of each of those currents. Often, there is.

Finally, when you can get in position above the pool, fish its main section again with the down-and-across presentation. This is a good time to use a lighter color jig, and maybe one slightly larger—something that will imitate a small baitfish.

There is virtually no kind of water in a stream that you can't fish effectively with a jig. In that regard, this really is a lot like fly fishing with nymphs or streamers because you can vary your presentation simply by changing positions or adjusting the weight of your offering. It's a killer approach.

Spinners

Throughout this book, I suggest that, all things being equal, your personal confidence is often the single most important element that determines success or failure on a given outing. With confidence, you're going to fish a given area with a given bait more carefully and thoroughly; in the process, you inherently increase your odds of catching fish.

I mention that because inline spinners are my confidence baits for trout. This style of artificial is the one that I prefer using over jigs, crank-baits or even subsurface flies like nymphs or streamers. They all work, and work well. But just like those friends of mine who swear by nymphs on flyrods, I swear by spinners on UL gear and am usually able to keep up with them or any other angler on the stream.

Spinners are my "go-to" baits when all else fails on a trout outing. That being said, I know that if I don't have much luck on spinners by the end of a fishing day, I can predict with fair certainty that the trout just weren't very active.

You might be able to say the same thing if you prefer nymphs on a flyrod or jigs or crankbaits. The point here is that, for me, spinners are the trout lures I have the most confidence in, and so will fish the most efficiently and effectively for the longest period of time.

This fishing faith in spinners is founded in my earliest days as an angler, when I was able to catch trout regularly on spinners while others were taking them on bait like salmon eggs and worms. For me, the appeal of spinner fishing was the fact that there was always some kind of

Better Than Flies

One of my most vivid spinner memories involves a truly wild, stream-raised rainbow on the Slatyfork section of the Elk River, West Virginia's longest river, in Pocahontas County. Funny thing is, I wasn't fishing spinners that day.

I had my flyrod along, and my fishing buddy, Jim Galusky, was flat-out kicking my behind. I just finished casting dry flies over a nice, long, rocky run with not even so much as a bite when I decided to stop fishing for a while and start paying attention to what Jim was doing.

His 1/4-ounce (7-g) gold Panther Martin had barely

splashed down when, seemingly out of nowhere, I saw a brilliant red shape explode from behind a rock and inhale the lure. A minute later, we were both admiring more than a foot (30 cm) of Slatyfork rainbow; a fish every bit as colorful as any you'd find in Big Sky Country out West.

I had drifted a dry fly over the same spot just a few minutes earlier. Maybe if I had switched to a nymph, I could have been the one to enjoy the feel of that spunky trout on the end of my line. Maybe.

All I know is that it showed me again why I'd rather fish spinners than nymphs or any other style of wet fly there is. For me, they just flat-out work.

The best way to fish this spot—with the current moving left to right—is to cast just on the far upstream sides of the boulders and retrieve the spinner fast enough to get it just behind each rock. Then, move it a little more downstream with each cast until you have thoroughly fished the slack water and current edges associated with each of the three exposed boulders.

action, even if it was just me casting and cranking. I didn't have to just sit there, next to an outfit with some kind of bait lying on the bottom.

Maybe I had an attention-deficit disorder before anyone had a name for it. Whatever the reason, I had to be doing something, not just sitting there waiting for the fish to bite. I had to go after the trout.

Early catches reinforced my approach, and I was hooked deeper than any trout I ever fooled. It wasn't until after I finished college and had a chance to begin exploring streams in West Virginia's Monongahela National Forest that I realized how effective spinners could be on trout—and not just hatchery-raised rainbows that were stocked by the DNR in streams like Glady.

I believe a major reason for my kind of faith is the fact that, over the years, I've learned to adapt my presentation to what the water offers.

Where to Fish

Just about anyone who fishes spinners learns to use them with a cast across and slightly downstream. This kind of presentation allows the lure to wobble across the currents and offer a good look to the fish. But it's not the only look that triggers strikes.

I'm going to mention something now that probably has happened to you more than once if you fish spinners. That is, you'll be casting to an area when you either see a fish slash at your lure without hitting it, or you feel a trout just bump the lure. How many times, when something like that has happened, have you chalked it up

to just missing the fish and moved on?

When I have a trout strike like that, I don't consider it a missed opportunity. Rather, I look at it as an aggressive fish revealing itself to me. As such, the challenge then becomes one of getting the bait back into the strike zone in such a way that the trout will actually take it.

Let's say I'm standing along the edge of a nice long run. It's fairly deep, maybe halfway up my thighs at its deepest point. There are plenty of rocks strewn across the stream bed, offering any number of likely hideouts for trout.

I begin with the across-stream cast. After a few throws, a trout darts out from behind a rock halfway across the stream to slash at the bait, but misses it, and moves back toward where it came from. For me, this is an exciting event. I know the fish is there, and I know it wants to eat. Because it only slashed at the lure, it didn't feel a hook. I have every reason to expect a strike if I can just give the bait a little different look.

My first move is slightly downstream. Once repositioned, I make a cast that will bring the bait into the strike zone from above, more closely resembling natural food tumbling downstream with the current. In this situation, my goal is to crank the reel as fast as I have to in order to get the spinner blade moving while keeping a tight line. In this presentation, I'm often fishing the bait faster than many anglers would ever consider. But time after time, it pays off. Active fish hit spinners hard when they're moving downstream like this. There's never any hesitation. But that's not to suggest that every trout you "roll" as described above will automatically attack a lure presented in this fashion.

If your downstream retrieve doesn't work, try reversing it before you give up on a trout you've seen. That is, position yourself upstream of the fish's holding lie, and make a cast that will permit you to retrieve the lure right over the top of the trout—not just under the surface, but as close to the bottom as possible. Something about this crawling kind of retrieve sometimes triggers strikes.

My general approach to fishing spinners is probably best described as "open-minded." Admittedly, I usually start out with the traditional presentation that involves casting across the stream and retrieving the bait as it swings across and slightly downstream from where it lands.

If I roll a trout, however, things change. I try as many different presentation angles as I can before giving up on a trout and moving along. This approach has led to catching more fish more often; it will for you, too.

Color Options

As to spinner colors, silver and gold are hard to beat. Ever since I tried one five years ago, my most productive spinner of all has been a traditional Panther Martin—a gold spinner blade above a black body with yellow spots, with no fly dressing on the treble hook.

Using this lure in 1/16-, 1/8- and 1/4-ounce (1.7-, 3.5- and 7-g) sizes, I've taken native, wild and stocked brook, rainbow and brown trout in a variety of weather and water conditions. If spinners are my "go-to" trout baits, then this is my "go-to" spinner. It's true that I have taken trout on other colors, especially either gold or silver lures with fly-dressed trebles in yellow or orange. Green spinners also produce well for me— after an angling buddy totally out-fished me with one.

The late Leslie Lovett, who spent his professional life photographing drag races and racers for the National Hot Rod Association, loved fishing even more than he loved those hot rods and their drivers. Bass, pike, trout, muskies, walleyes; it didn't matter. Leslie just fished.

He was visiting one summer when we checked out Crane Creek, a fishery in southwest Missouri that is home to a beautiful strain of wild rainbows. I fished a gold Panther Martin with an orange fly, then switched to a silver lure with a yellow fly when the first one didn't produce. The second didn't, either.

Leslie, on the other hand, caught and released a bunch of rainbows up to 15 inches (38 cm). We were fishing about 50 yards (45.5 m) apart, and I finally had to go see why he was taking trout and I wasn't.

"This is my special spinner," he said, holding up a version of the popular Rooster Tail lure in what its maker, Worden's, calls green coach dog. That day, on that stream, that dog could hunt up some trout!

Ever since then, I've used that green coach dog with good success when my other colors wouldn't produce. Again, it goes back to confidence. Whatever works for you does so in part because you fish it with the confidence born out of past success. It's a key when fishing spinners or any other bait.

Panther Martin Regular Gold, 1/8 oz.

Panther Martin Orange, 1/8 oz.

Panther Martin Regular Dressed Silver, 1/8 oz.

Panther Martin Dressed Chartreuse Blade, 1/8 oz.

Luhr-Jensen Bang-Tail, 1/8 oz.

Mepps Aglia Ultra Lites, 1/18 oz.

Crankbaits

Trout hit crankbaits, too. They love 'em. The best news about that is that there are more options at your fingertips today than at just about any other time in fishing history when it comes to UL plugs.

Minnows have been favorites of live-bait trout anglers for generations. Today, those of us who prefer artificials have many options when it comes to crankbaits that mimic the look and movement of the small live baitfish that trout hit best.

And in recent years, at least one manufacturer has given all of us UL "hardware chunkers" an opportunity to enjoy a special brand of late-summer fishing that previously had been reserved only for flyrodders or bait users. That is, we can fish terrestrials.

For that, you can thank PRAD-CO, the Arkansas-based company that makes and sells a number of crankbait lines, including Rebel. And under that brand name, the company has introduced a whole series of plugs that imitate terrestrial insects like grasshoppers and moth larvae.

These baits are effective any time that the real-life species they imitate are available to trout. Usually, that means from August through late September; although it's apparent that they will produce throughout the season.

Most of the time, however, I prefer to imitate stream life with my crankbaits. Using small Rapalas, the Tiny Trap version of the Rat-L-Trap lipless crankbait and other UL minnow imitations is one option. But if I have a "go-to" crankbait for trout, it's another model from Rebel—the Wee-Craw.

Specifically, this is the 77 series of 1/10-ounce (2.8-g) crawdad crankbaits that have

One trick for fishing crankbaits for trout is to stand upstream and use a slow retrieve up into the very point where a fish is holding.

been on the market for roughly two decades. I started using them while living in Kansas in the mid-1980s, and once made a special trip to the Slatyfork section of the Elk River while back home on summer vacation just to see how the stream's wild rainbows and browns would react to them.

Oh, my! The first trout I caught, a foot-long (30-cm) brown, was one of several that came after the lure on my first cast. Maybe they'd never seen the bait before. But for whatever reason, they came after it time and time again.

Where to Fish

These days, a Wee-Craw still works just as well. And there's one kind of presentation that I save it for: I think of it as my "when all else fails" presentation. It involves the very heads

of pools and riffles in freestone trout streams.

These are spots where water tumbles over rocks at a waterfall that could be just a few inches to a foot or two (30 to 60 cm) tall. Often, trout will take up ambush spots literally under or adjacent to those falls. These are among the toughest trout to catch on any stream simply because their hideouts are so problematic to fish.

I like to stand just above the falls with one of those crawdad crankbaits and flip it a few feet (meters) below where the water tumbles over the rocks. Then, using as slow a retrieve as possible, I work the lure up into the very point where the water is splashing down from above. Fish dart out from the slack water under the falls or right next to them to smash the bait. There's never

any hesitation with this kind of strike. It's a trick that will add a fish or two for you on practically every outing.

Beyond this, there aren't any magical secrets to fishing UL crankbaits for trout; and that's what makes them so inviting. This is the epitome of casting and cranking. The lure does all the work. Your goal, simply, is to get the bait in the strike zone and keep it there as long as possible.

With that in mind, I generally reserve my crankbait fishing for pools and falls. The latter is a specialized presentation. The former, especially with sinking lures like a small countdown Rapala, gives me a chance to fish the deepest parts of pools thoroughly.

I also believe that crankbaits are the best of the big-fish baits when it comes to UL trout fishing. Trout don't grow to be measured in feet (meters) and weighed in pounds (kilograms) by wasting a lot of energy. The big ones use the best hideouts, which generally are found in the deepest parts of a stream. They take advantage of the largest meals they can find.

Crankbaits give you the chance to fish those big-fish lairs with artificials that mimic the biggest natural meals any trout will encounter. That makes them hard to pass up.

Rebel Big Ant, 1/8 oz.

Rebel Teeny Wee-Crawfish, 1/10 oz.

Rapala Countdown, 1/8 oz.

Rebel Crickhopper Popper, 3/16 oz.

Rebel Suspending Ghost Minnow, 1/8 oz.

Jerkbaits for Big Browns

Around the country, you'll find fisheries that are home to truly large trout. Mostly, they're browns and they sometimes grow to weights of 25 pounds (11.25 kg) or heavier! Lake Taneycomo, in southwest Missouri, is one such lunker lair.

And it was there that I learned of a bait that you can use whenever you have a chance to fish a spot with large browns. It's a bass bait, and one that many trout anglers would never, ever think of trying. Specifically, it's a rainbow trout–colored, soft-plastic jerkbait.

Maybe your favorite fishery

doesn't grow very big browns. Maybe a 5-pounder (2.25-kg) is a trophy where you like to fish. That shouldn't keep you from trying this lure and this technique. After all, big browns eat rainbows, and they're as opportunistic as any other predator. Give them a lure that looks like a smallish rainbow in trouble, and they're going to attack it.

This presentation works best on lakes or large pools in streams. The latter should offer some decent areas of slack water, where the bait can be fished as it is intended—without much regard to the current. You also can start it out in the slack water of a pool and jerk it quickly across the main current, using quick, short twitches to make the bait look like a rainbow really

struggling in the swiftest part of the flow.

As is the case with other kinds of lures mentioned in this section, you have plenty of choices these days in soft-plastic jerkbaits. They have become staples of the bass angler's arsenal, and many manufacturers make a version in a rainbow trout color.

They are simple to rig: Run the point of your hook through the bait's nose, bring it out of the lure quickly, twist the hook around and take the point through the body as if you're going to Texas-rig it for weedless fishing. But instead, run the point all the way through the mid-section of the lure's body and leave it exposed.

It's a big-fish bait that could help you land the trophy of a lifetime.

15 Minutes of Fame

Several years ago, newspapers in the area carried the account of a local angler who frequented the first mile or so of Taneycomo below the outlet of Table Rock Lake. This is the physically smallest section of the waterway, and the area that most resembles the traditional trout streams many anglers are most used to fishing. But even here, the water is big and deep.

This fisherman started throwing bass-size Slug-Go baits in a rainbow trout color. He fished them just as if he were after bass. He rigged them without weight, on a large bass hook, and fished them in or just under the surface film with an erratic, jerky retrieve that imparted the look of a wounded trout.

Big browns, it turned out, couldn't resist them. He made the paper when he hooked and landed a 25-pounder (11.25 kg) on the lure!

Chapter 9

Trolling Tiny Baits for Big Fish

This chapter is about an ultralight fishing technique that many anglers might never consider. But when opportunity presents itself, there's no reason not to seize it and run.

You may have to change your trolling approach a little because, in this case, slow is best. But the bottom line is simple: You can troll using ultralight gear and baits, and it will be more effective than you can imagine.

Where to Fish

One of the most important elements of enjoying success with this brand of ultralight fishing involves locating the best places to fish. Experience has taught me that there are

some keys to trolling locations, and they vary from lake to lake. All of them seem primarily to be depth related.

Out West, for example, many of the region's largest impoundments are extremely deep and gin-clear. But those factors don't rule out ultralight trolling. As you move east into the heartland, you find lots of lakes, big and small. That is, they are much shallower, and often are at least slightly stained at their most clear. Unless you're in the northern tier of states in this region, the majority of impoundments are man-made, regardless of their size. And they generally are never more than 50 feet (15 m) deep, and usually not more than 30 feet (9 m) deep.

Moving farther east, you find the most diverse collection of trollable impoundments. There are plenty of man-made lakes, but also a fairly good number of natural impoundments. Their depth and relative clarity vary from location to location, and that can present a challenge for first-time or infrequent angling

visitors—especially those who want to try their hands at trolling ultralight baits.

The first key to success involves not getting caught up in trying to analyze things too much. Keep two things in mind when trying to figure out the places most likely to get your tiny trolled baits in front of fish willing and eager to bite: structure and natural forage.

The premier spots, like those flats on Clinton Reservoir, are the ones that provide anglers with access to schools of baitfish relating somehow to nearby structure. At Clinton, it was the meandering main channels of the lake's two major arms. Those channels were adjacent to fairly expansive flats near the major point in this wishbone-shaped impoundment. The baitfish seemed to stay close to or over the breaks, where the flats dropped off into the deeper channel. At Clinton, I learned quickly to concentrate my trolling passes on this structure break, which meant keeping the boat generally over 16 to 22 feet (4.8 to 6.7 m) of water.

Troll near structure or cover like weedlines and submerged humps. Start with the shallowest-running version of the crankbaits you want to troll. Cover the upper reaches of the fish's "strike zone" first, then switch to a deeper-running plug if the fish doesn't come up to attack the lure.

Structure

Among the unique features of many northland and western impoundments are the submerged humps that rise to only 10 to 20 feet (3 to 6 m) under the surface from much deeper water. These are exceptional areas for trolling because many species of gamefish use them, and so do the forage species they regularly feed on.

Another structural element you'll often find on impoundments are stands of submerged weeds and vegetation. These are predominantly found throughout the South and Southeast, and on some natural lakes in the North. When you find spots like these, key in on them.

The best approach is to either troll along the edges of the weedlines if their tops are less than 4 feet (1.2 m) deep, or move right over the tops of them if there's enough open water to allow your lures to dive to their natural depths and work properly without constantly hanging up in the underwater growth.

The latter definitely is the preferred method because it lets you get your lures right over the best ambush and holding hideouts of the gamefish in the lake. Baitfish generally use weeds like this eagerly, so the combination is a good one.

If shallower stands of weeds force you to focus on the edges, you should further restrict most of your attention to natural breaks along the weedlines. Those include main or secondary points and the mouths of bays and smaller coves—all of the places that predators like to hang out and lie in ambush for easy meals.

You can thank your fellow anglers for another kind of trolling hot spot: the area between the shore and man-made fish attractors that usually are sunk within easy casting range of shorebound fishermen. When it comes to trolling, these are among the most underfished spots because most anglers simply don't think about the possibilities of taking fish in what amounts to a funnel.

The structure itself is not the only reason gamefish will be found nearby. Forage also is drawn to the man-made cover, and predators need that forage to survive. They sometimes take up ambush points in water slightly shallower than the fish attractors. This is especially true on overcast days with low levels of light penetration, the best times to make these closer-to-the-bank trolling passes.

And if all else fails, make some passes through areas that strike you as good trolling targets, and use your fish finder to locate bait. The species you're after are very likely to be close by and a trolling pass or two away from landing in your live well.

TROLLING TINY BAITS FOR BIG FISH

When to Fish

To be successful, you still have to be in that right place at the right time. Experience over the years has left me believing that, for reasons I can't pinpoint, late afternoon and early evening seem to be the best times for ultralight trolling. No doubt, there is a combination of factors that makes this true. It must relate to the way baitfish move around an impoundment, and there has to be a connection between the amount of light penetration and the aggressiveness of the gamefish.

I've learned that I can start earlier on cloudy, less bright days. I also learned that when the sun sets, my trolling for that day is done. It seems as if Nature flicks a switch when the sun dips below the horizon. You can continue to catch fish by other means into the evening and through the night. But for some reason, trolling success absolutely dies on the last rays of a setting sun. At least, it always has for me.

And for some reason, outings at dawn or through the early-morning hours haven't ever been as consistently successful as those trolling trips that started after the sun had peaked and was on its way toward the western horizon. Of course, success during afternoon/evening trips has been so consistent over the years that it's been tough to spend a lot of time dragging ultralight lures through likely spots over morning coffee.

My point is that, admittedly, I probably haven't spent enough time on the water during the first half of any given day to conclude with certainty that morning trolling doesn't work. But that's because I do know, without question, that afternoon/evening trips are productive. And that makes them really attractive—especially to anglers who enjoy getting out during the spring, summer and early fall for a few hours after work during the week.

For that reason, my recommendation is that you focus your ultralight trolling on the later hours of daylight on any outing.

Lure Options

I'd like to tell you that there is some hot, secret, better-than-all-the-rest combination of size, shape and color that is the ticket to ultralight trolling success. The bad news is, there isn't. But if you think about it, that might really be good news.

What I mean is, you won't find a list in this book of lures that don't take fish when trolled. I haven't used any that failed on a regular basis. Sure, there have been times when the

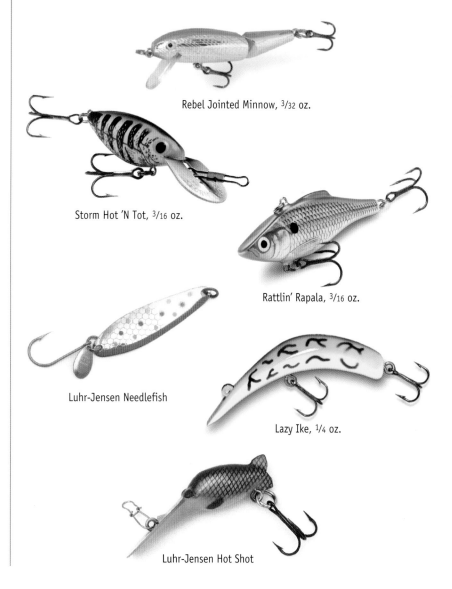

Rebel Jointed Minnow, 3/32 oz.

Storm Hot 'N Tot, 3/16 oz.

Rattlin' Rapala, 3/16 oz.

Luhr-Jensen Needlefish

Lazy Ike, 1/4 oz.

Luhr-Jensen Hot Shot

Choice of lure color is based on water clarity and the existing light conditions. Stay with natural colors on bright days; when light begins to fade, go with bright colors like chartreuse.

fish have been neutral or negative on a given day, resulting in few, if any, strikes. But when they were biting, they hit all the lures I've trolled. And my criteria is fairly broad: A bait has to weigh no more than 1/4 ounce (7 g), and it has to be designed to work the way it's supposed to when trolled. In other words, I've never trolled topwater poppers or walking baits, but any plug intended to work below the surface, with or without a diving lip, has fooled fish when I've used it.

Are some more effective than others? Sure. Among the best are the shad-size lures, and lures 2 to 3 inches (5 to 7.6 cm) long that resemble crawdads. The action of the latter entices strikes—not the fact that it looks like a crawdad. After all, you just don't tend to see crawdads meandering around in open water, say, suspended 6 to 8 feet (1.8 to 2.4 m) deep over 20-plus feet (6 m) of water.

A key element of these baits' effectiveness, it seems, is their design, which in many respects is a lot like the traditional FlatFish-style wiggling crankbaits. I mention that because

my success with the crawdad baits led me to try the FlatFish-style family of plugs, and every one I experimented with was quite effective. So, in some respects, trolling gives you a chance to expand your arsenal of lures to include some styles that many of today's anglers might otherwise overlook— especially on species that are home to lakes in the southern half of the U.S.

Depending on the specific brand and model of the lure you intend to troll, you may be faced with decisions regarding whether to use the normal or deep-diving version. I think you should always start out with the normal, standard version of the bait in question. In the most general of terms, that means you'll be trolling a bait that probably won't run deeper than 6 feet (1.8 m). Some are designed and intended to run even shallower. That has never been a problem for me.

During one night of discovery on Clinton Lake, the schools of baitfish my buddy and I spied on the boat's electronics were routinely suspended deeper than our baits would normally run. But the crappies

and white bass hit them. On later trips, we also had large-mouths and walleyes hit them. It seems as if those predator fish relating to roaming schools of bait are often more positive and, as a result, more aggressive. They come up to take what looks like an easy meal. I suspect that one reason is the bait looks like it's wounded because it's moving erratically and it's separated from the pack. That's a natural ambusher's delight!

As you might guess, the relative water clarity and amount of light help dictate what colors I troll. It's a fairly simply equation, really. Go brighter on darker days; more natural on sunnier days.

You can even fine-tune your color approach on those bright days because light penetration changes as the shadows lengthen from late afternoon into evening. On those first outings on Clinton, I learned that the gamefish would react best on bright afternoons to baits in shades that matched the forage fish. Shad colors, blue-over-silver and black-over-silver, were the choices.

But I soon learned to check when the sun would set on the day of a trolling trip because, like clockwork, the fish would slow way down in reaction to the natural baits during the last half-hour before sunset. At that point, a switch to fire tiger, chartreuse or other bright colors would get the action going again in a hurry.

If a chance to troll presented itself on a dark, dreary, overcast day, it was those brighter colors from the get-go. Black-over-gold baits also work well on this type of outing.

Trolling Speed

A final thought on lures and trolling them: You can fine-tune their performance underwater by changing line size, which is something professional walleye and bass anglers have been doing for more than a generation. This is especially important to keep in mind when trolling, even at the slow speeds I'm about to suggest for ultralight crankbaits.

Regardless of the speed of your retrieve or your troll, line diameter causes resistance to the water, and it affects how deep your lure will dive and run with proper action. The rule of thumb is that the heavier the line, the shallower your bait will work. It's a function of line diameter. Thicker line offers more resistance. Going from, say, 8-pound (3.6-kg) line down to 4-pound (1.8-kg) line when trolling will have an impact on how deep your bait will run. It might only be slight but, sometimes, a slight difference can be major when it comes to how fish react to your lure.

Now, when it comes to ultralight trolling, speed is even more important. I only need four letters to spell success when fishing like this: S-L-O-W. Can I tell you a precise speed to troll ultralight baits at? Yes. And no. That is, I know exactly how fast I need to be going to have the best chance at catching fish; but I never measured it so I can't provide a number. The truth is, it probably varies by bait because of the specific actions of the lures.

What I learned early on was a simple rule of thumb for ultralight trolling: You should only be going as fast as necessary to impart the action the lure was designed to perform with. Any faster only exaggerates the action or wobble, and fish don't seem to get excited by it. Any slower, and the lure just isn't working the way it's supposed to.

If you want to quickly learn the art of judging the right trolling speed when using ultralight crankbaits, there is one thing you'll have to watch closely and pay the most attention to—the tip of the rod. It is going to tell you everything you need to know in order to make the most of every trolling pass you complete on a given outing.

Here's the way I start, and continue, every trolling pass I make with ultralight lures: I cast the lure using an average motion, which usually would put it 25 to 30 yards (23 to 27 m) behind the boat. Then,

Watch the rod tip when trolling to make sure the speed of your boat is keeping the right action on the lure.

starting the trolling motor, I crank the reel handle 4 to 6 times, which helps the bait get down to its intended running depth. Then, I put the rod in a gunwale-mounted holder, or just hold it in my hand, paying attention to the vibrations being transmitted up the line to the tip of the rod. Usually, the lure is working with a fairly strong vibration. At this point, I slow down.

As soon as the rod tip stops moving, I begin easing the speed up until the vibration just barely starts. At that point, the lure is at its running depth and is displaying the action built into it. I know from experience that's all the faster I need to go to catch fish. In fact, moving quicker seems to diminish the lure's ability to entice strikes.

Without question, the best success I've enjoyed trolling like this has been on those days when I could troll into the wind. The breeze's resistance gave me a chance to really fine-tune my trolling speed and actually maintain it more consistently over the course of a long pass.

In some of the other situations mentioned, like passing over flooded humps or moving through the "corridors" between the shore and submerged man-made fish attractors, your lures inherently will be in the strike zone for less time. In these cases, it's best to adapt a concept bass fishermen have used for years. That is, start your trolling pass far enough away from where the fish are so that, by the time your lure arrives, it is doing exactly what it's designed to do.

TROLLING TINY BAITS FOR BIG FISH

A New Approach

A few years ago, one of my fishing buddies had joined me for a late spring outing on Clinton Reservoir, a U.S. Army Corps of Engineers flood-control impoundment in Douglas County, Kansas, about 45 minutes west of greater Kansas City. We'd heard that walleyes were active on Clinton's flats, and set out to troll crankbaits for them.

Before setting baits in the water, we made a pass on either side of Clinton's main point, looking for structure breaks, the main channel and any fish that might be moving about. We got excited at the number and size of the baitfish schools showing up on the fish finder. The fish seemed to be lurking around them hoping to pick off quick and easy meals. They weren't as deep as we thought, either. Although the main concentrations of baitfish were only 4 to 6 feet (1.2 to 1.8 m) beneath the boat, they were suspended over 18 to 25 feet (5.5 to 7.5 m) of water, and seemed to be relating to the meandering main channel.

After doing our "recon" and figuring out the best trolling baits, we put out some medium-diving crankbaits and stickbaits, then began moving along with the fish finder as our guide. One pass turned into several, and the late afternoon turned into early evening without any of our baits enticing a bite.

So, on a lark, I reeled in the stickbait and traded the medium-action spinning outfit for an ultralight rig I had in the rod box. I quickly attached a tiny crawdad-imitation plug, lobbed it behind the engine, and made another pass over those schools of fish.

We hadn't gone 50 yards (45.5 m) when the whippy tip of the ultralight rod snapped down, then stayed almost taut, transmitting the energy of the fish that had struck the little lure. This fish's fight was fierce; and when I finally got my first glimpse at a real slabside crappie of almost 2 pounds (0.9 kg), I got excited.

I turned to my fishing partner, Joe, to ask whether he'd seen the fish yet. I got my answer as I spied him laying down the rod he'd been trolling with for one about as light as mine. "Do you have any minnow baits that small?" he asked. "I'm curious to see whether I can get a crappie to hit one."

Knowing my addiction to ultralight fishing, Joe's question was supremely rhetorical. While I was boating and unhooking the big white crappie, then popping it into the live well, he was rummaging through my tackle box, and came up with a smallish floating/diving shad imitation in a natural hue.

His lure was in the water only a few seconds after mine, and our efforts were quickly rewarded with a double hookup. But this time, I had a chunky white bass more than a foot (30 cm) long, and Joe got a crappie. For the next couple of hours, we loaded up on perfect-eating-size whites and the largest crappies either of us had ever seen on Clinton by trolling ultralight crankbaits.

What neither of us could say was whether our encounter had been a fluke. So we hurried back to Clinton as soon as our schedules would permit, hitting the water at about the same time a couple days later. Instead of messing with walleyes and the larger lures we thought would fool them, we started out with the ultralight gear and the action picked up right where we'd left it less than 72 hours earlier. By the time we returned to the ramp to head home, each of us knew that we'd discovered a unique approach to trolling that paid off big time.

Chapter 10
Fly Fishing

The largest trout I've ever caught hit a dry fly I was fishing on a 5-foot 3-inch (1.6-m) flyrod. I made a roughly 50-foot (15-m) cast over a deep run in a wide West Virginia river on a sunny Sunday afternoon in 1981.

Of course, that 19¼-inch (49-cm) rainbow didn't know I wasn't using a 9-foot (2.7-m) rod with a 6- or 7-weight line to reach its hiding place.

Back then, more than twenty years ago, fly fishing offered the ultralight angler few choices. That's not the case today. You can even find outfits built to handle a 0-weight flyline. You can't get any lighter than that, but you can catch big fish on this kind of gear. I've also had great luck with bass and panfish.

Trout

I suspect that at least some anglers reading this book consider the term ultralight fly fishing a little oxymoronic. Fly fishing inherently involves tackle lighter than some would use on the same fishery for the same species.

When it comes to trout fishing, my rules are simple: If I'm fishing dry flies, I want the shortest rod I can find—a concept that flies in the face of the sport's traditional thinking. For nymphs, streamers or other wet flies, I switch to a longer rod (for reasons I'll discuss in a minute). But it's not very heavy; a 4-weight line is as big as I go.

Nothing changes the game like switching to a short rod. The longer your casts, the more flyline that remains on or in the surface film during every presentation. When fishing dry flies, your goal is a drag-free drift. That is, your fly should dance downstream with the current seemingly not attached to anything. It should look as if it is just another insect resting in the surface film as it unsuspectingly drifts right over a trout ready to rise for an easy meal.

On some of the largest trout streams in this country, there will be times when you have to make casts longer than 50 feet (15 m). But for most flyrodders in most dry-fly situations, 50-foot casts are very few and far between. So don't think for a minute that trying a flyrod shorter than you are will complicate your casting. Plain and simple, it won't.

It will, however, force you to become expert at mending line. That means you must handle the flyline that floats along during every presentation so that your fly's drift is as long as possible without drag. This is most important when you're positioned at least somewhat across the stream from the spot you want to fish.

Casting Strategy

Let's say you're wading up an average-size eastern freestone stream, or a smallish western flowage. In each cast, the river or creek is 40 to 50 feet (12 to 15 m) wide. You're wading up the left edge because it's fairly shallow. But there's a nice, deep run across from you, one that you've taken trout from on previous visits. You know it's a spot you can't afford to pass.

Then, just as you're trying to figure out your best presentation, a nice brown rises just where you thought there ought to be a fish.

If only you could just take a few steps back downstream and to the right, you simply could make a traditional upstream cast. That would take most of the challenge out of your line-mending issue. But as almost always is the case, the stream isn't going to let you get away with it. For one thing, there's a healthy wild rhododendron hanging over the water just below. For another, the water gets fairly deep in a hurry.

Even if you could manage to wade into upstream-casting position without getting wet, that rhododendron won't let you false-cast, even with a short rod, because you need to have too much line out. Your fly would get hopelessly tangled in its branches. So you have to go after the fish from across the stream.

In this kind of situation, my approach is to make a cast that drops the fly onto the surface at least a few feet above where I saw the trout rise. I then make an upstream mend as soon as it touches down. If I have enough room to do so, I actually have a foot or two (30 or 60 cm) more of line out than I need to reach my casting target, which allows me to add some slack when I cast.

This is going to take some practice, but you can do it anywhere. When I practice casting in the yard, I use an old, beat-up fly and simply cut the barb off the hook. It won't stick into anything, but it will get you very close to the actual on-stream feel.

Pick a casting target. Use a clump of grass, or maybe even set a paper cup out there, and practice making a cast that will drop your fly 12 to 18 inches (30.5 to 46 cm) beyond the cup. When you have enough line out to do that, pick it up and start false-casting, but now concentrate on your target. As you make your final casting stroke, lift your rod tip slightly to stop the fly's forward momentum and cause it to drop right down.

It may take several attempts, but you'll soon be able to judge when to stop the line to put your fly on that target. Now look at the slack flyline lying in front of you. Making this kind of cast in an across-stream presentation will automatically enhance your ability to achieve a drag-free drift because of that slack.

On the water, you'll have to add one more step to the process: It's that upstream mend mentioned earlier. As soon as your fly touches down, make a small circle in an upstream direction with your rod tip. If you're casting to the right, make the circle counter-clockwise, in the upstream direction. If you're casting to the left, reverse it to a clock-wise motion.

Just remember that it's an upstream mend, so the movement should always cause your slack line to jump slightly upstream. Doing this also lengthens your drag-free drift, regardless of how much current is available. It's relative, of course. In the best of situations, you make the cast and mend once, and your fly gets right over the trout, which rises and takes it. More often, however, you'll probably have to make upstream mends a few times on each presentation.

These are the skills you'll need to make the most of fishing dry flies on super-short rods. Anyone who learns to flycast can enjoy plenty of action with a 9-foot (2.7-m) rod because the extra length helps keep more line off the surface. You don't have that luxury when using rods in the 5- to 6-foot (1.5- to 1.8-m) range, so you have to learn to add slack in your casts and mend line upstream to opti-mize every presentation.

Just don't get frustrated on your early outings with a short rod. These casting and mending tips involve your sense of feel. If you commit to making a short rod work for you, it won't be long before all of this becomes second nature.

Probably the best way to learn is to visit some of the smaller streams you enjoy fishing; flows that don't get much wider than 20 to 30 feet (6 to 9 m). Most native brook trout fisheries are this size, and many streams that get stocked during the late winter and spring are not much bigger. They'll be hitting dry flies before the stocking season ends, so you'll have your chances.

Make the most of them by practicing in the yard, then hit the water knowing that you need to pay more attention to your slack line than you would if you had a much longer rod in your hand. Remember: The trout won't have any idea how long your flyrod is, and they won't care. If you get your fly to drift over them naturally, they're going to rise and take it.

Covering Water

Fly fishing soon becomes an exercise in covering water. One of the things that still amazes me about trout is how many different kinds of holding lies they use. I can't even begin to tell you how many fish—and many of them really nice ones—I've spooked over the years simply by not fishing thoroughly enough.

Dry flies make it so easy to do that because you can cover every little spot you see. Some fly anglers might disagree, but my experience suggests that you can cover any trout stream more effectively with a dry fly than with any other fly, or lure, for that matter.

If you don't believe it, try this

Dry Flies

March Brown

Red Quill Spinner

Nymphs

Dark Hendrickson Nymph

Marabou Midge Larva

Terrestrial

Foam Ant

Attractors

Royal Wulff

Mickey Finn

Wooly Bugger

little experiment the next time you go out: When you can safely do so, wade into the middle of the stream you're fishing and take a good, long look upstream. Look left, then slowly scan across to the right. Along the way, note any spot where you believe a fish might be hiding.

Now, start casting your dry fly to all of them you can reach. Work left to right again. Cover every little current tongue, every little eddy created by a rock in the stream.

Could you have done that same thing with a nymph? Chances are good your answer is no. More often than not, the need to get your fly down and/or the shallow nature of some potential fish-holding lies make subsurface fishing much more difficult when you want to be as thorough as possible. At least, they do for me.

Even with the shortest of dry-fly rods, I know that by learning to add slack in my casting, and by mending line as necessary, I can drift a dry fly over any spot in the stream that I choose to. Fishing doesn't get any more thorough, or effective—when you take your time. When fish-

ing dry flies, I can't emphasize that enough. Trout are going to be in places you might walk right past. Take the time to make a few extra casts. Cover the best-looking locations first, but don't pass up any spot.

And, as mentioned earlier, take the time to break up larger streams and rivers into sections. When I can do so, I like to wade into the middle of a long run, then break it up into thirds. I'll fish everything to my left first; then cover the center; and I'll finish with the spots to my right. Taking this approach will help you no matter where you fish. It's a lot easier to cover water thoroughly this way, and it helps you avoid going right past a fish you otherwise might entice to rise.

When you do decide to go subsurface with your fishing, switch back to a longer rod and lighten way up. Your fly fishing will be more fun and less tiring every time. My logic for suggesting the long rod is simple: When you're fishing any kind of wet fly, your line is going to telegraph strikes to you. With or without a strike indicator of some sort, you're paying

The style of fly fishing—nymph or dry fly—not the size of the stream, dictates what length of flyrod to use.

attention to even the slightest of movements in your line, and reacting with a hookset.

As a result, keeping as much line off the water as possible is paramount to your success, no matter what the weight of the outfit you're fishing with. So while I prefer the challenge of super-short flyrods when casting dries to rising trout, I believe a rod at least 8 feet (2.4 m) long is very important to your success with nymphs, streamers and other wet flies. I just don't believe it has to be very heavy.

My cutoff is a 4-weight. Even an outfit that light will permit you to cast bulky, weighted nymphs like Wooly Buggers without any trouble. And they are good bets, especially during the early and late parts of the season, when water temperatures are lower and, as a result, trout are less aggressive.

Leaders

Regardless of what time of year you're fishing, or whether you're casting dry flies on a short rod or fishing nymphs on a 9-foot (2.7-m), 3- or 4-weight outfit, you also have to take your leader into consideration. It's as important as any other element of your gear because unless it tapers properly, you're not going to cast or present your flies very effectively.

When fishing dry flies, you can use long leaders with short rods. On all but the smallest, tightest of native brook trout streams, I use a leader at least 9 feet (2.7 m) long on the little 5-foot 3-inch (1.6-m) rod I talked about earlier in this chapter. For me, the key to casting longer leaders on this rod has been to always make sure I had a foot or two (30 or 60 cm) of flyline outside the

rod tip when I started false casting. Remember that the fly-line's weight is what permits you to cast. Getting a little of it going quickly will help you pick up a longer leader much more easily with a short rod like this.

When fishing nymphs and other subsurface flies—with or without a sinking or sink-tip line—proper leader taper is just as important. It may be more important because it's going to help you get that fly down to where it needs to be as quickly as possible.

No matter how big or small your fishing tackle is, your primary goal in using it always is the same: You want to get whatever bait you're fishing into the strike zone as quickly as possible on every cast, then keep it in the strike zone as long as possible.

A properly tapered leader does that by turning your fly over on the cast and helping it to hit the water first. By the time your line settles, that usually means the fly has already gotten down to or near the bottom, and it's drifting along as naturally as possible with the current. That's what you want, and a leader that's not correctly tapered just won't make it happen.

Match the Hatch

I've read articles in which flyrodders have talked about simply using a fairly short piece of line as a leader when fishing subsurface. You can do it, but it's not nearly as effective as keeping everything as balanced as possible—and a tapered leader is critical to that balance. I absolutely believe it's more important than even matching the hatch. I've proven to myself time and time again

A Cool Head

Remember that big trout I caught on the little rod? That rainbow hit a size 10 Royal Wulff dry fly. The pattern is known as an "attractor" because it doesn't match anything in nature. Its body is made of peacock, with a red cummerbund of sorts in the middle. It's a hair-winged version of the traditional Royal Coachman pattern, which has been around for generations.

I choose the hair-wing variant, one of a series of dry flies developed and named for late fly fishing legend Lee Wulff, because I can see it well—a whole lot better than I can see most "match the hatch" patterns. Add the fact that the pattern is a fish-catching machine, and I have all I need...

...Except for a cool head. I can tell you without reservation that when that big rainbow came up, hit my Royal Wulff and rolled on the surface—tipping me off to its size—I pretty much came unglued. Then, when the big trout felt the hook, that little rod practically bent in two and stayed that way for most of the fight.

Thank goodness for Jack Bell, the man who taught me to fly fish. He was standing right beside me when the fish hit. He saw it was a big one, too. And he started coaching me immediately.

"Stay cool. Don't get too excited," he said, between laughs. I know I was funny, babbling pretty much nonstop about how big the fish was and whether I was going to get a chance to touch it.

"If it wants to run, let it run," Bell said. "Just keep pressure on it. And when it stops, try to get some line back. Just keep doing that, and the fish will wear out quicker than you might think."

He was right. What amazed and excited me the most about this whole episode was the way that short little Fenwick fiberglass rod really shone with its ability to wear the trout down.

In those few minutes of playing, then landing, that big trout on that little rod, I realized that this kind of action didn't have to be rare. I learned that, as long as I had the room to cast and could mend line floating on the water when I needed to, I could take trout almost anywhere on this stubby little flyrod.

From that moment on, I knew that I didn't have to think ultralight only when I was using spinning gear. The same concepts could apply to my fly fishing, too, and they'd work.

that you don't have to get that technical to catch trout.

If, however, the hatch-matching concept appeals to you, go for it. Especially through the heart of the season, when water temperatures and on-stream insect activity are at or close to their best, you can do very well using flies that imitate the larval stages of insects you know inhabit the stream you're fishing.

But you also can take what I call the "impressionistic approach," which involves using less-specific-looking flies. Their general look can mimic more than one species of aquatic insect.

Although some veteran fly-rodders might disagree with me, I believe that some kinds of wet flies have been lost, in recent years, in the rush to fish nymphs practically all the time. Streamers don't get as much attention these days; neither do other traditional wet flies that are not nymph patterns.

More than two decades ago, I read Sylvester Nemes' first book on soft-hackle wet-fly patterns. For me, that underlying theme has never been lost. Nemes has updated *The Soft-Hackled Fly: A Trout Fisherman's Guide*. It's available online at www.Amazon.com, and likely

will be found in most fly fishing specialty shops that carry books on the sport. It truly is a classic.

Flies like the soft-hackle patterns are simple to tie and to fish. For me, they are the epitome of what fly fishing can be—a simple, yet effective way of taking trout.

Don't get me wrong. I understand and respect the viewpoint of those for whom the sport involves the challenge of matching specific insects in specific situations on specific streams. I'm just suggesting that it doesn't have to be so complicated.

Bass and Panfish

Have you ever seen an angler flycasting off the raised front deck of a go-fast, tournament-style fiberglass bass boat? Me neither; although I've done it. During the postspawn period in late spring (and continuing into early summer), when all three black bass subspecies (large-mouth, smallmouth and spotted) readily take topwater plugs and poppers, flyrodders can enjoy some very exciting action. Add the concept of lightening up, and you've got all the makings for some great fishing memories.

Although some would argue that the following suggestion is not really lightening up, I wouldn't go much below a 6-weight outfit if I were going to cast the largest of deer hair popping bugs for bass. Given that my "standard" rig for such fly fishing is an 8-weight, I submit the No. 6 is a lot lighter, and will handle those large flies. At first, casting those bulky, fairly heavy bugs on what many folks consider to be an "average" trout outfit (a 6-weight) likely will feel awkward.

And I'm not going to suggest that you try to make casts much beyond 25 to 30 feet (7.5 to 9 m). But within those parameters, you can take bass this way without a lot of trouble.

From Shore or Boat

Even on a small farm pond, really covering the water means making fairly long casts. I'm talking about often reaching out 50 to 60 feet (15 to 18 m), which gets close to two-thirds of the standard 90-or-so-foot (27-m) flyline off your reel and flying back and forth over your head.

When you're fishing from the bank, no matter how large the body of water, stick with rods in the traditional longer lengths. Doing so will help you make longer casts because the line is going to be at least a foot or two (30 or 60 cm) higher when you false-cast, and that can make a big difference. Trying to fish with a rod in the 5- to 6-foot (1.5- to 1.8-m) range is going to be difficult at best—unless you can get in a position that somehow elevates you slightly above the ground behind you.

I can think of only one situation in all my years of ultralight fly fishing when that was a reality. My longtime friend Jim Givens has a small pond next to his eastern Kansas home, and its dam drops right off to a large pasture below. That pond often stayed within a few feet (meters) of the top of the dam, which meant I could cast flies a long way without worrying about hanging up on anything behind me. Unfortunately, a setup like that is the exception and not the rule when fishing from the shore.

For me, nothing beats fly fishing for bass and panfish from a boat. You generally don't have to worry about what's behind you when false-casting a popper or other surface fly, and you can position the boat to make the most of every presentation by getting just the right casting angle and distance.

When fishing subsurface flies for these warmwater species, I generally don't do much more than make roll casts from the boat. Using the trolling motor, I get in position to make relatively short casts.

One thing some flyrodders

Fly fishing from a boat is hard to beat for bass and panfish. You can eliminate practically all the hassles associated with snagging flies behind you, and you can maneuver very precisely to make just the right presentation. This can be especially important with top-water poppers and deer-hair flies.

don't seem to understand is that false-casting isn't done for style or aesthetics. You false-cast simply to help surface flies stay dry.

You don't need to false-cast when fishing wet flies. At most, you might have to get all the line out behind you to load it up for your next presentation. But beyond that, there isn't any need for casting motions that don't get your fly back into the strike zone.

When it comes to bass and panfish, that strike zone often is along a shoreline with at least a slight incline—one where I can make the cast, then let the fly slowly fall down

Bass Flies

Panfish Flies

Bunny Fly

Black Wooly Worm

Deer-Hair Popper

Dahlberg Diver

Cork Popper

Yellow Cork Popper

Gold-Ribbed Hare's-Ear Nymph

along the bank toward the bottom. Fish often hit flies presented like this on the drop, just as they would a plastic worm or grub.

In shallow coves or on main-lake flats, I try to make casts that will get my fly a few feet (meters) beyond whatever the structure is that I'm fishing. It might be some rocks, an old stump or a brush pile. I let the fly settle to the bottom, then slowly crawl it along past the spot where a fish will be lying in ambush—if one is there.

Flies

There are plenty of flies on today's market that will permit this kind of fishing, which I liken to fishing the plastic worm mentioned earlier. I tend not to complicate my subsurface fly fishing for bass and panfish because, in all honesty, there's no need to. And this is the kind of fishing where I'm

most likely to use a sinking or sink-tip line. When you lighten up, the line itself helps you get relatively smaller, lighter flies down to the fish more quickly.

If you are predisposed to tie flies, you could take a light-wire, long-shank hook in, say, a size 6 and quickly come up with an excellent minnow imitation that would be light enough to cast even on a 3-weight outfit. Really.

You simply wrap some gold or silver Mylar around the shaft of the hook, then tie in some strands of maribou or synthetic flashabou material at the head of the fly. In a minute or so, you'll have a fly that offers flash and movement through the water.

Will it win any beauty prizes? Doubtful. Will it catch fish? Most likely. That's another beauty of fly fishing to me. You can make your approach, even when it comes to tying effec-

tive flies, as simple or as complicated as you want. It's all up to you.

And when it's up to me, simple is better. Some anglers love to tie flies. I don't. I want to fish. I do enjoy the satisfaction of catching fish on flies I've created, but I don't want to spend as much time creating them as I do fishing them, let alone more. So my flies rarely look very pretty. But they work. Yours can, too.

Or you can simply buy some flies and have more time to spend catching fish. I think that's a valid trade-off.

When it comes to panfish, you have a lot more choices in flies than some anglers realize. Many often think only of fairly small poppers when talk turns to flyrods for bluegills, crappies, perch and sunfish.

Standard trout streamers work very well, and they're available in sizes that definitely allow you to lighten up significantly. Some readers are going to laugh at this next statement, but it's true: Anywhere I have the room to make a cast, I know I can use streamers like a Muddle Minnow, Mickey Finn or Wooly Bugger to catch panfish on my 2-weight trout rod! Talk about fun—you can't imagine it until you try it.

Throughout the summer months, terrestrials also are patterns that will take panfish and even bass on occasion, especially from farm ponds in pastures that become July and August homes to grasshoppers, crickets and the like. Throw in those traditional poppers, and you have quite an arsenal.

If you're strictly after bass, large streamers or leech patterns are dynamite subsurface bets, and crawdad imitations are very effective when you're fishing rocky structure. Using a sinking or sink-tip line will give you a chance to cast flies of this type on outfits as light as a 3- or 4-weight and have a good chance for success.

From a boat, you can use a supershort rod to fish topwater poppers. You should be able to make casts of 30 to 40 feet (9 to 12 m) even with a rod shorter than 6 feet (1.8 m). Fishing for bass this way is among the most exciting angling experiences you can enjoy.

Yes, I know. Casting larger flies on short and very lightweight outfits like this can feel—and actually be—awkward. Shorter, tapered leaders (say, in the 7-foot/2.1-m range) will enhance your ability to cast large, fairly bulky flies. And there's no reason you can't practice ahead of time. Spend some time in the backyard

learning the feel of big flies on little rods. If you do, you're going to get pretty good at it.

My approach with wet flies is to fish from a boat whenever possible, and to use the trolling motor to get in position for precise, short casts around structure and along points and other shoreline. If you're doing little more than a roll cast, which is the goal here (getting your line out of the water and, using a windmill kind of motion, getting the fly back for another presentation), it's not going to feel a whole lot different than fishing a weighted nymph on a trout stream.

What is going to feel different is the fight of bass and panfish on ultralight fly gear. They're going to seem even more fierce and spunky than normal. Playing and landing them successfully involves remembering one word: easy. It's just like playing a big trout or any other fish. Take your time; don't get in a rush. If a fish wants to run, let it. Keep a tight line, keep your rod tip high, and let the rod do most of the work—like it's supposed to.

Hooks and Leaders

Before you head out on a bass or panfish excursion with your flyrod, take some time to sharpen the hooks on your flies. Achieving good hooksets can be difficult to begin with when you're fly fishing for these species. Add the challenge of ultralight flyrodding tackle, which has less power than the more traditional outfits used for bass and panfish, and you have even more reason to want your hooks absolutely as sharp as they can be.

Although I've made only

brief mention of leaders in this section on bass and panfish, you shouldn't let that mislead you into thinking that they're not an important part of this ultralight challenge. In fact, I can argue that, especially with surface flies, proper taper might be the most important element of your approach. If you decide to try the things I've suggested in this section, you're going to have to use a leader that will get a large fly to turn over well on lighter and shorter flyrods. As mentioned, I believe leaders in the 7-foot (2.1-m) range will help you accomplish that. And fortunately, bass and panfish don't become as leader-shy as finicky trout on a clear mountain stream.

Most commercial manufacturers are making and selling knotless, tapered leaders in the 6- to 8-foot (1.8- to 2.4-m) range that are designed to turn over large topwater bass bugs efficiently. You can find them with tippet sections as light as 6 pounds (2.7 kg).

Make no mistake, hooking a keeper-size bass on a bass bug, using a short flyrod with a 6-pound tippet, you're going to enjoy a challenge and the fun of ultralight fishing that's as good as it gets.

For panfish, you can even use the shorter (say, 7-foot/ 2.1-m) trout leaders in 3X or even 4X. They'll turn over the wet flies and smaller poppers you'll be fishing just fine on a 3- or 4-weight rod.

AFTERWORD

Confidence.

Few things impact your fishing more, and even fewer are tougher to grasp. Ultralight fishing inspires confidence. If you take nothing else from this book, take that concept.

For more than three decades, catching fish on lures smaller than I should have been using—and casting them on the lightest gear possible—made me confident, then kept me that way. It's improved all of my fishing.

Knowledge definitely is powerful, and the kinds of ultralight fishing covered in this book have taught me a lot. Most importantly, my success in using the gear, baits and techniques I've shared has taught me that I can catch fish any ol' way I care to. You can, too. And my hope is that, after reading everything this book covers, you'll want to try at least some of what I've discussed.

It will work for you because it works for me. I'm not a genius. My fishing talent is average at best. I lose fish when I shouldn't; catch them when I shouldn't. I'm no different than you—unless you don't fish ultralight.

Then, I'm only different inasmuch as I've thought outside the fishing box. I've dared to try some things others thought were outlandish. And I've stayed persistent when my gut told me that what I was trying just had to work.

There isn't anything magical or mystical here. I wish I could take credit for some innovative new approach to one of humankind's oldest pursuits—the hunt for and, with use of deception, capture of living things that can provide physical nourishment or, with gentle treatment and a quick release, plenty of spiritual nourishment.

But I can't. This is just about challenging yourself to be the best angler you can be. Going ultralight will get you there. Enjoy the trip.

MANUFACTURER SOURCES

Abu Garcia
800-228-4272
www.abugarcia.com

Arbogast Lures
www.arbogastlures.com
479-782-8971

Bass Pro Shops
www.basspro.com
800-227-7776

Berkley
800-237-5539
www.berkley-fishing.com

Bill Lewis Lures
www.rat-l-trap.com

Blakemore Lure Company
417-334-5340
www.blakemore-lure.com

Blue Fox Lures
800-874-4451
www.bluefox.com

Bomber
479-782-8971
www.lurenet.com

Booyah Bait Company
479-782-8971
www.lurenet.com

Cabela's
800-237-4444
www.cabelas.com

Cajun Line Company
800-347-3759
www.cajunline.com

Charlie Brewer's Slider Company
800-762-4701
www.sliderfishing.com

Cotton Cordell
479-782-8971
www.cottoncordelllures.com

Creme Lure Company
800-527-8652
www.cremelure.com

Daiwa Corporation
562-802-9589
www.daiwa.com

Dardevle
888-771-8277
www.eppinger.net

Drifter Tackle Company
419-662-3933
www.driftertackle.com

Eagle Claw
720-941-8700
www.eagleclaw.com

Fenwick
877-336-7637
www.fenwickfishing.com

Garcia-Mitchell
877-336-7637
www.fishmitchell.com

G.Loomis, Inc.
800-456-6647
www.gloomis.com

Heddon Lures
479-782-8971
www.heddonlures.com

Johnson
877-502-6482
www.fishjohnson.com

Kalin Company
760-344-2550
www.kalinlures.com

Lazy Ike Lures
479-782-8971
www.lurenet.com

Lindy
218-829-1714
www.lindyfishingtackle.com

Luhr-Jensen & Sons
800-535-1711
www.luhrjensen.com

Mann's Bait Company
800-841-8435
www.mannsbait.com

Maxima America
714-850-5966
www.maxima-lines.com

Mepps
715-623-2382
www.mepps.com

Okuma Reels
www.okumafishing.com

The Orvis Company
888-235-9763
www.orvis.com

P-Line
415-468-0452
www.p-line.com

Panther Martin
800-852-0925
www.panthermartin.com

PowerPro
www.powerpro.com

PRADCO
479-782-8971
www.lurenet.com

Quantum
800-588-9030
www.zebco.com

Rapala
800-874-4451
www.rapala.com

Rebel
479-782-8971
www.rebellures.com

Redington
800-253-2538
www.redington.com

Reef Runner Fishing Lures
419-798-9125
www.reefrunner.com

Riverside
479-782-8971
www.riversidelures.com

St. Croix
800-826-7042
www.stcroixrods.com

Sage Manufacturing
800-533-3004
www.sageflyfish.com

Seaguar Fluorocarbon
www.seaguar.com

Shakespeare Fishing Tackle
800-347-3759
www.shakespeare-fishing.com

Shimano American Corporation
949-951-5003
www.shimano.com

Slug-Go
203-237-3474
www.lunkercity.com

Smithwick
479-782-8971
www.smithwicklures.com

Spiderwire
877-502-7743
www.spiderwire.com

Stanley Jigs, Inc.
936-876-5713
www.fishstanley.com

Storm Lures
800-874-4451
www.stormlures.com

Stren
866-447-8736
www.stren.com

Strike King
901-853-1455
www.strikeking.com

Strike On! Lures
877-634-8170
www.strikeon.com

Suick Lure Company
715-623-7883
www.suick.com

Terminator
800-944-4766
www.terminatorlures.com

TUF-Line
970-241-8780
www.wfilament.com

US Reel
314-962-9500
www.usreel.com

Worden's Lures
509-854-1311
www.yakimabait.com

Gary Yamamoto Custom Baits
800-645-2248
www.yamamoto.baits.com

Yo-Zuri America, Inc.
888-336-9775
www.yo-zuri.com

Yum
479-782-8971
www.lurenet.com

Zebco
800-588-9030
www.zebco.com

CONTRIBUTING PHOTOGRAPHERS

Bill Buckley
Bozeman, MT
© Bill Buckley/www.thegreen
agency.com: p. 33

Mark Emery
Ocala, FL
© Mark Emery: pp. 22, 49T,
102–103

Tim Lilley
Athens, GA
© Tim Lilley: pp. 7, 40, 41, 42, 47,
80, 86B, 87, 97, 103B, 113, 122

Bill Lindner Photography
Minneapolis, MN
© Bill Lindner/blpstudio.com:
pp. front cover, 3C, 6, 21, 37T,
39, 55, 58, 60, 62B, 63, 64T, 66,
69, 100, 119

David J. Sams
Dallas, TX
© David J. Sams/davidjsams.com:
pp. 19T, 30, 44, 53T, 67, 70, 89,
95, 96, 118

Dusan Smetana
Bozeman, MT
© Dusan Smetana/www.thegreen-
agency.com: pp. 3L, 4, 82, 90,
104, 110, back cover B

Dale C. Spartas
Bozeman, MT
© Dale C. Spartas/spartasphoto.com:
pp. 112, 114

Doug Stamm
Prairie du Sac, WI
© Doug Stamm/stammphoto.com:
pp. 46, 65T, 88

(Note: T=Top, C=Center, B=Bottom, L=Left,
R=Right)

INDEX

A

Abu Garcia, 13
Arbogast Lures, 31

B

Bait, 84
Baitcasting reels, 15
Baitcasting rods, 11
Bass Pro Shops, 12, 13, 14, 16, 31, 55, 75
Bass, 44–57, 66, 118
  Crankbaits, 55
  Jigs, 48
  Soft plastics, 50
  Spinners, 52
  What other fish tell you, 47
  Where to fish, 53
Berkeley, 16, 17, 24, 56, 75
Bill Lewis Lures, 29, 30, 31, 55, 56, 81, 100
Blakemore Lure Company, 43, 51, 65
Blue Fox Lures, 26, 27, 32
Bomber, 29, 56, 80, 81
Booyah Bait Company, 26, 53, 63, 79
Buzzbaits, 79

C

Cabela's, 12, 16, 19, 20, 55, 75
Cajun Line Company, 16
Carolina rigging, 51
Casting, 113
Catfish, 82–89
  Bait, 84
  Flatheads, 86
  Fly fishing, 89
  Reels, 83
  Rods, 83
  Where to fish, 84

Charlie Brewer's Slider Company, 50
Color, 52, 99
Cotton Cordell, 29, 56
Crankbaits, 28, 55, 66, 80, 100
Crappies, 47, 58–69
  Crankbaits, 66
  Jigs, 59
  Spinners, 63
  Spoons, 68
  Where to fish, 68
Creme Lure Company, 51
Current, 40

D

Daiwa Corporation, 13, 14, 15, 29, 56, 74
Dardevle, 32, 68, 81
Drifter Tackle Company, 80

E

Eagle Claw, 9, 11, 12, 15

F

False-cast, 114
Fenwick, 12, 17, 18, 19, 20, 89
Flatheads, 86
Flies, 113–121
Fluorocarbon, 17
Fly fishing, 18, 89, 112–121
  Bass, 118
  Flies, 120
  From shore, 118
  Hooks, 121
  In a boat, 118
  Leaders, 121
  Match the hatch, 116
  Panfish, 118
  Trout, 113

G

G.Loomis, Inc., 12, 20, 72
Gaines Phillips, 56
Garcia-Mitchell, 17, 91
Global Positioning System, 38

H

Hatch, 116
Heddon Lures, 31, 56
Hideouts, 37
Hooks, 61, 93, 121
Hybrid, 17

J

Jerkbaits, 102,
Jigs, 48, 59, 91
  Natural look, 48
Johnson, 13, 32, 63, 65, 68

K

Kalin Company, 26

L

Lakes, 37, 64
Lazy Ike Lures, 107
Leaders, 117, 121
Lindy, 77
Line, 16, 18, 72
  Fluorocarbon, 17
  Hybrid, 17
  Monofilament, 16
  Superline, 17
Luhr-Jensen, 32, 81, 99, 107
Lures, 22–33, 76, 107
  Crankbaits, 28
  Soft plastics, 24
  Spinners, 26
  Spoons, 32
  Topwater baits, 30

M

Mann's Bait Company, 52
Maxima America, 16, 75
Mepps, 26, 32, 81, 99
Monofilament, 16
Muskies, 70–81
  Buzzbaits, 79
  Crankbaits, 80
  Lines, 74
  Reels, 74
  Rods, 72
  Soft plastics, 76
  Spinnerbaits, 78
  Spoons, 81

O

Okuma Reels, 13
Orvis Company, 19, 20

P

Panfish, 47, 58–69, 85, 118
  Crankbaits, 66
  Jigs, 59
  Spinners, 63
  Spoons, 68
  Where to fish, 68
Panther Martin, 26, 27, 63, 97, 99
Pike, 70–81
  Buzzbaits, 79
  Crankbaits, 80
  Lines, 74
  Reels, 74
  Rods, 72
  Soft plastics, 76
  Spinnerbaits, 78
  Spoons, 81
P-Line, 16, 17, 75
Ponds, 37, 64
PowerPro, 17
PRADCO, 55
Premier, 11

Q

Quantum, 8, 11, 12, 14, 15

R

Rapala, 9, 10, 12, 28, 29, 55, 73,
  80, 100, 101, 107
Rebel, 28, 29, 31, 55, 56, 57, 80,
  100, 101, 107
Redington, 20
Reef Runner Fishing Lures, 55
Reels, 13, 20, 72, 83
  Baitcasting, 15
  Spincasting, 13
  Spinning, 14
Riverside, 24, 62
Rod action, 10
Rods, 7, 18, 72, 83
  Baitcasting, 11
  Spinning, 9
Rooster Tail, 26, 27, 99

S

St. Croix, 11, 12, 20, 73
Sage, 20
School fishing, 60
Seaguar Fluorocarbon, 17
Shakespeare Fishing Tackle, 9, 12,
  72, 73
Shimano American Corporation,
  13, 15
Silver Thread, 16, 17
Slug-Go, 52, 103
Smithwick, 31, 56
Soft plastics, 24, 50, 76
Spiderwire, 17, 75
Spincasting reels, 13
Spinnerbaits, 26, 53, 63, 78, 97
Spinning reels, 14
Spinning rods, 9
Spoons, 32, 68, 81
Stanley Jigs, Inc., 49
Storm Lures, 31, 56, 80, 107
Streams, 40, 63
Stren, 16, 75
Strike King, 49, 78
Strike On! Lures, 78
Structure, 38, 106
Suick Lure Company, 80
Superline, 17

T

Tackle, 7–21, 72, 83
Terminator, 31, 78, 79
Texas rigging, 51
Topwater baits, 31
Trolling, 104–111
  Lure options, 107
  Speed, 109
  Structure, 106
  When to fish, 107
  Where to fish, 105
Trout, 90–103, 113
  Browns, 102
  Color options, 99
  Crankbaits, 100
  Jerkbaits, 102
  Jigs, 91
  Spinners, 97
  Where to fish, 94, 98, 101
Tuf-Line, 17

U

U.S. Reel, 13

W

Water, 30, 34–43, 115
Worden's Lures, 56, 99
Worms, 51

Y

Yamamoto, 49, 50, 77
Yo-Zuri, 16, 17, 29, 55, 75
Yum, 24, 52

Z

Zebco, 13

Creative Publishing international

is your complete source of How-to information for the Outdoors.

Available Outdoor Titles:

To purchase these or other Creative Publishing international titles, contact your local bookseller, or visit our web site at
www.creativepub.com

The Complete
FLY FISHERMAN™